SEP 09 — Dec-09 = 6

W9-BQY-937

HAT
HEADS

HAT HEADS

1 MAN + 2 KNITTING NEEDLES =
50 FUN HAT DESIGNS

Watson - Guptill Publications, New York

GLEN ELLYN PUBLIC LIBRARY
400 DUANE STREET
GLEN ELLYN, ILLINOIS 60137

TROND ANFINNSEN, *aka* KNITKID   *Photography by* KLAUS NILSEN SKRUDLAND

Editorial Director: Victoria Craven
Senior Acquisitions Editor: Julie Mazur
Editor: Linda Hetzer
Art Director: Jess Morphew
Designer: www.goodesignny.com
Production Director: Alyn Evans

First published in 2009 by Watson-Guptill Publications,
an imprint of the Crown Publishing Group, a division of Random House, Inc., New York
www.crownpublishing.com
www.watsonguptill.com

Text copyrights © 2009 Trond Anfinnsen
Photographs on pages 10-11, 16, 17, 30, 31 copyright © 2009 to Steinar Engelsen;
those on pages 34, 35, 42, 44, 50, 104, 164, 166 copyright © 2009 to Ingvild Aarsland;
all other photographs copyright © 2009 to Klaus Nilsen Skrudland

Library of Congress Control Number: 2008942462

ISBN: 978-0-8230-9236-9
All rights reserved.

Printed in China

1 2 3 4 5 6 7 8 9 / 17 16 15 14 13 12 11 10 09

CONTENTS

800 HOURS OF KNITTING

HatHeads is the result of roughly eight hundred hours of knitting over a twenty-month period. This lunacy resulted in something like two hundred unique, one-of-a-kind hats, each designed for a particular friend or family member in Norway, where I live, and all given away for free. All of the hats were photographed on their recipients by my close friend Klaus, who started to photograph at approximately the same time I began knitting. We called our joint project, oddly enough, the Knitting Project.

The main purpose of this book is to inspire you to knit one of the hats presented or—even better—to design one of your own. Most of my two hundred hats are shown somewhere in these pages, though only fifty are presented with patterns and instructions. This winnowing-down was necessary so it would be possible for you to carry this book home from the store.

If you are new to knitting, this book will help you go from no-knitting-skills-at-all to able-to-make-a-fairly-decent-hat-of-your-own. Super beginners (or anyone who needs a refresher) should turn to the Help Desk chapter on page 156 for instructions on basic-knitting stitches and a couple starter hat patterns to get you on your way. Knitters who already know the ropes can dive right in and use that chapter for a refresher as needed.

The people I've knit hats for are a wide and varied group—old, young, male, female—comprising a mosaic of personalities. With each pattern and photographic portrait, I've written a short sketch to try and capture the essence of each one, not quite succeeding in resisting the urge to caricature just a little bit. Hopefully I've not only managed to share how each inspired his or her pattern, but also to introduce you to a warm and wonderful group of people.

I still get questions about making hats for people, and I still do, because I like doing it. But technically, my and Klaus's part in the Knitting Project is over. That's where you come in. This book is an invitation to continue the knitting project in your own world, whether by making one of the fifty patterns, or by using the tips on page 168 to design a personalized hat for someone special. Who wouldn't love a warm gift made especially for them?

I hope these hats and people inspire you to knit, to give, and to appreciate the quirks and gifts of friends and family surrounding you, wherever you call home. ❖

STARTING TO KNIT

I started knitting in the winter of 2006. Like most things in life, it was something of a coincidence. It all started on a bus trip from my hometown of Stavanger, Norway, to the Austrian ski resort of Kitzbühel. A colleague of mine, who was also the trip's organizer, had discovered that I possessed a bus driver's license. So there I was, driving the bus to Austria.

As we drove, one of the other organizers was killing time in a way that caught my attention. He was knitting. I studied him as he worked. He looked so calm. Normally, he was much more of an up-and-down person. He was very enthusiastic, always talking, joking, laughing, organizing, going through passenger lists, studying the map, playing guitar, and a whole lot of other things. But when he was knitting, he was at rest, gathering energy and losing himself in thought. Knitting seemed like a kind of meditation, directing his energy inward. I think that was the aspect that intrigued me the most.

After a week of skiing, I came home and immediately bought the materials to make a hat. I had only a vague idea of how to do a basic knit stitch. I had to learn everything else: casting on, purl stitch, knitting on circular needles, and so on. In other words, I had the knitting skills of a ten-year-old Norwegian kid after his first knitting lesson in school.

I spent a couple of evenings making my first hat, and I was proud as a rooster with it. On my second hat I started using purl stitches, and putting ribbing along the bottom. As I made more hats, I added new techniques: using different colors, mixing knit and purl stitches in exciting ways, cabling, using different types of yarn and different sized needles, and so on. I created my patterns as I went.

THE FIRST HAT

This is the first hat I knitted. It actually turned out remarkably nice and even, considering it was my first hat. Maybe I was made for this? The hat is made out of alpaca yarn, and there is no ribbing at the bottom because I had not yet discovered purl stitches.

THE UGLY HAT

It might be quite arrogant to call this *the* ugly hat, thus implying that I have made only one ugly hat. But actually, that's what I think. I may have made some mediocre hats, but this is the only one I consider simply ugly. When I started this hat I had only a few colors left in my pile of yarn, and decided that that limitation should challenge me. When I design hats I try to find a good balance between strong, dark colors and brighter colors. How I ended up putting dark brown and dark red in the middle of the white, with light blue at the bottom, I still don't understand. You will never see me wear this hat again.

THE KNITTING PROJECT

Knitting turned out to be exactly what I imagined it would be after studying my traveling companion. When I was knitting, I was relaxed. My thoughts traveled anywhere and everywhere. (Maybe at this point in my life I needed lots of meditation.) Before I knew it, I had created quite a large assortment of hats. Obviously, I did not need all these hats myself. So I started giving them away to friends and family. My knitting then also gradually evolved in the direction of designing each hat specifically for one person. So each time I started on a new hat, I had one particular person in mind. After having knit hats for quite a lot of people, I realized that my work was sort of just disappearing in all directions, and I decided to start documenting the

hats and their recipients in photographs. That was when I contacted my close friend Klaus Nilsen Skrudland.

Klaus had just purchased a camera and was totally immersed in light, focus, composition, and just about every aspect of photography. I asked him about making simple portraits of all the people who had received hats. But, knowing Klaus, nothing can be done simply. He attacked the task with total dedication, and we spent every spare minute shooting portraits around the region. We soon developed the idea of making the portraits visually cohesive as a series: They are all taken from the same distance, from the front, and with the subject centered. They all have more or less single-color backgrounds, and all were cropped

to a square format. Thus, the "Knitting Project," as we called it, was born.

Over the next two years, I designed and knit—and Klaus photographed—more than two hundred hats for friends, family, and other people in our area. We received press in the newspapers and on television in Norway, starting with a front-page article in our local newspaper, and coverage by the local television station that led to a story on one of the most popular and longest-running national television shows. We heard from people all over the world on Flickr.com, where we posted many of the portraits.

Knitting was as meditative for me as I thought it would be. I get totally immersed in knitting a hat and the hours just fly by.

Here are some of the hats I made for members of my family during my knittingmania period when I was knitting two or three hats a day. Left to right are my sister Gunhild, my girl-friend Åse, and my nephew Kaj Andre.

Here's the mayor of Stavanger. His personal adviser had seen my hats on the Internet and he agreed to involve the mayor in the project. We arranged a meeting at City Hall (opposite), with newspaper and local television reporters by our side, and I handed over this hat, which very clearly states who the head of the city is.

THE JOY OF THE GIVE

Throughout the project, and particularly once my hats reached a certain level of quality, people started asking, "Why don't you start selling your hats?" My gut feeling has always been not to sell them, but to give them away. It simply gives me a good feeling to give gifts and receive gratitude and surprise in return. The simple fact that, one: you have made the gift yourself, two: that it has obviously taken a considerable amount of time to make, and three: that the gift is specially designed for the one who receives it, makes it extra special to give. The receiver will know that you have actually been sitting for hours working for and thinking about him or her. It's great. ▓

My family were, obviously, among the first ones to receive hats from me. This is my mom and my dad.

The Midtun family (including mom on page 36) has been heavily involved in this knitting project from the start. I think they were all happy with their hats.

Since I was knitting so many hats, I had lots of scraps of yarn left over. Here's me in my favorite hat made from these scraps. The easiest way to make a hat like this is simply to tie together lots of short strands, and to wind this length into a large ball. You can use all sorts of colors and yarn weights together.

SELF PORTRAITS

I made it a habit to take a self-portrait after completing each hat. Immediately after finishing a hat, I put it on my head and pointed my digital camera directly at myself, trying each time to make the photographs look as similar as possible. As the collection of these photos grew, I thought that the mosaic of portraits looked kind of cool. The pictures presented here are a series made by my friend and photographer Klaus—and are of a much better quality than my original set. ❉

SEARCHING FOR AN IDENTITY

After making and giving away quite a lot of hats, I started thinking in terms of bigger concepts. I wanted a name, a logo, an identity.

Initially, I used the name Elektrofant. This is Klaus's electronica band, which I also was a member of at one time. Both Klaus and I liked the idea, so I started knitting Elektrofants. But then, many knit Elektrofants later, Klaus changed his mind.

Then I came up with the UFO. This abbreviation seemed just funky enough for my hats. I sketched a simple UFO, ending with a Space Invader-ish figure. I used the acronym not for "Unidentified Flying Object" but for "Uniquely Funky Outfit" and thought I had a winner. Unfortunately, I found out that there was a denim brand called UFO.

At this point, all funky flying objects and electronic elephants were out, and I just continued calling myself Knitkid, which is the name I had always used on the Internet. My friend Per Kåre Reiersen made a logo out of the word, and presented it to me on my fortieth birthday.

Look closely at this stack of hats, and you'll see some of the labels I had made with the Knitkid logo, designed by my friend Per Kåre.

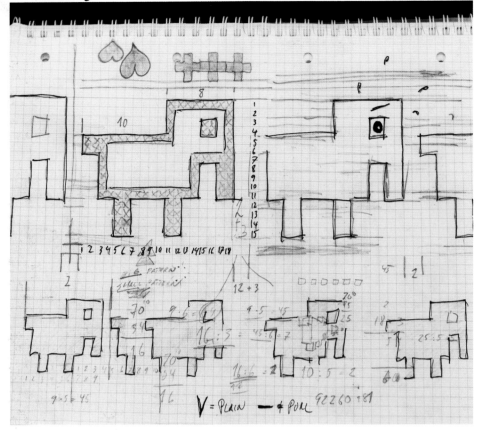

Here is the page in my design notebook showing the process of creating an electronic elephant in knit stitches.

KNITKID™

The Knitkid logo, created by Per Kåre.

I had labels made using the Knitkid logo. The head of the factory that makes these labels told me he would make them for free if I made a hat for his daughter. So I did.

Members of my family wear hats with many designs, some of which are variations on electronic elephants and UFOs, my first attempts at creating a logo for my knitting. Left to right are my nephew Martin, my niece Gyda, and my niece Sina.

NORWAY, THE LAND OF FJORDS AND KNITTING

If you ask the average Norwegian about knitting, you probably won't get much response. This is partly because Norwegians aren't known as big talkers. But more so, knitting is such an ordinary part of Norwegian culture that we don't think much about it. It's like eating, sleeping, or driving. It doesn't seem special because everyone does it, and it has always been around. I don't know if Norwegians knit more than people of other nationalities, but all Norwegians are taught the basics

of knitting in school at a young age. Many women in Norway have brought this art beyond the basic skills learned in school, and they knit sweaters, hats, gloves, and socks for their families all the time.

Here are stories of three very different people who illustrate for me this special relationship between Norway and knitting.

My girlfriend and I have a friend named Lene whom I've known for years. She has always knit *a lot*! I remember once when she was visiting us, I noticed that she was knitting, and I said: "Hey, you're knitting too!" My comment produced

strange looks from both Lene and my girlfriend. They both made it clear to me that she had been knitting practically forever. The point is that I had never noticed, until knitting suddenly had become an interest of mine. Knitting is just something you do when you are being social. It is hardly noticeable. This is the kind of knitting I have grown up with: mothers, aunts, sisters knitting. It is still very much a female activity. I cannot think of any other men that I know who knit.

This second story is a little more dramatic. David Aleksander Toska is considered one of the top criminal minds in Norway. During the early morning hours

This photograph of a classroom in the 1950s shows almost every boy wearing a Norwegian sweater, probably knit by his mother, aunt, or grandmother.

on April 4, 2004, he led the biggest and most well-organized armed robbery in Norwegian history. With military precision and loads of weapons, he and his gang seized an entire city block in downtown Stavanger. They shot their way into a bank, killed one police officer, and drove away with millions. Stavanger was left in shock. One year later, Toska and most of his gang were arrested; he confessed to having organized the robbery, but denied responsibility for the police officer's death.

What does this have to do with knitting? During the trial, Toska did everything in his power to present himself as a respectable and trustworthy person. And his single most important tool was a traditional Norwegian knit sweater. He wore this sweater throughout the trial. It became his trademark, and the subject of lots of talk. Considering what he had done, it turned out that the sweater did not earn him very much sympathy at all. He received a long sentence, and faces years behind bars.

But if you had never heard the story, the sweater does make him look like a quite nice man, warm and trustworthy, doesn't it?

Another famous Norwegian associated with knitting is Hans Nielsen Hauge, who was born in 1771. As the story goes, one day when Hauge was in the field plowing, he suddenly felt the strong

Just after the robbery, Toska and his gang hid out in a shack next to my girlfriend's apartment. During the trial, my friend Klaus took this shot, from the window of her apartment, of Toska wearing his knit sweater, while he and the police were inspecting the different crime scenes.

Both the *lusekofte* I am wearing, with its traditional Norwegian pattern, and the *selbuvotte* or mittens, with another pattern common to Norwegian knitting, will keep me warm in our cold Norwegian winters.

presence of God. He immediately started preaching…and walking. Between 1797 and 1804 he walked great distances across Norway, stopping at farms and preaching about the joys of God, hard work, and sober living. While he was walking, he was—you guessed it!—knitting. He walked and knit, giving the socks he made to children he encountered along the way. I have never knitted while walking, but maybe I should give it a try?

For all the knitters in Norway, there are some knitwear and knitting patterns that are typically Norwegian, strong symbols of everything we think of as Norwegian, just like fjords, mountains, clean water, farms, good health, simplicity, and easy, old-fashioned living. The *lusekofte*, what you might call a sweater-jacket, knit in one of a number of traditional patterns, is the most Norwegian symbol of them all. The *selbuvotte*, or mittens, is another.

So knitting and Norway just go together. From the basics learned in school to the prodigious knitting skills of many Norwegian women, from the tales of a knitting evangelist to the wily manipulations of a notorious criminal, knitting is part of life in Norway. We live with knitting every day and everyone most likely has a piece of handmade knitwear—a scarf, a sweater, a pair of socks, or mittens—in his or her closet.

GETTING

STARTED

WHY KNIT, AND WHY KNIT HATS?

It is important to sometimes just sit down and do nothing. The amazing thing about knitting is that you can do it while you sit and do nothing. And what's special about knitting compared to other creative activities is that all the creative decisions, like choosing the color and the pattern, are made *prior* to the actual knitting. That means that you can actually be creative and productive while resting. It is the perfect meditation. You do not even need the television on. A radio in the background works, but total silence is amazing, too. Just sit down, let your hands work the needles, and let your thoughts wonder off to distant places. Before you know it you will be sitting there with your girlfriend's birthday present in your hands.

Hats are very easy to knit compared with other pieces of clothing. And a hat is a knitted item that deserves your artistic attention because it sits close to your face, which is the reflection of your personality. A hat is also very visible, the last thing you put on before going out, like the crown on your outfit.

This is also what makes knitting hats for other people so much fun. Which type of hat will fit that person? Which colors should you use? What should the pattern look like? When you give the person the hat you have knitted and see that it fits—and that he or she actually wears it a lot—you know that you have done a good job. ❖

YARN

Yarn is the most important choice you'll make in knitting, and the variety of yarns available feels boundless. Here's what you need to know about yarn to help you make your choices.

Fiber Yarn is available in natural fibers, such as cotton, linen, wool, silk, and mohair; synthetic fibers, such as acrylic, nylon, and polyester; and combinations of both.

Texture Yarn comes in all kinds of textures—smooth, bumpy, thick-and-thin, and twisted. If you are a beginning knitter, you may want to start with a smooth-textured yarn like the ones used in these hats so you can more easily see the shape of your stitches.

Color Choosing colors is a way of expressing yourself. Yarn is available in so many colors that you can easily find a color or combination of colors that you love. Use your color choices to make your hat uniquely yours.

Weight Yarn is classified by weight or thickness, from thin fingering yarn to bulky yarn. The Yarn Council of America has developed a standardized system for yarn weights, shown on the next page, with symbols that are used throughout the industry.

THE CRAFT YARN COUNCIL OF AMERICA'S STANDARD YARN WEIGHT SYSTEM

YARN WEIGHT CATEGORY	Super-Fine	Fine	Light	Medium	Bulky	Super-Bulky
SYMBOL	**1** SUPER FINE	**2** FINE	**3** LIGHT	**4** MEDIUM	**5** BULKY	**6** SUPER BULKY
TYPES OF YARN	Sock, fingering, baby	Sport, baby	DK, light worsted	Worsted, afghan, Aran	Chunky, craft, rug	Bulky, roving
NUMBER OF STITCHES IN 4 INCHES OF KNITTED PABRIC	27–32 sts	23–26 sts	21–24 sts	16–20 sts	12–15 sts	6–11 sts
RECOMMENDED NEEDLE SIZES (U.S.)	1–3	3–5	5–7	7–9	9–11	11 and larger
RECOMMENDED NEEDLE SIZES (METRIC)	2.25–3.25mm	3.25–3.75mm	3.75–4.5mm	4.5–5.5mm	5.5–8mm	8mm and larger

I get lots of inspiration for the hats I knit just by looking at all the wonderful colors of yarn available, and seeing how I can combine them in my designs.

MY YARN CHOICES

In this book I used only three types of yarn: Falk from Dale of Norway, and Smart and Alfa from SandnesGarn.

Falk is a 4-ply combed yarn in 100% pure new wool. It is machine-washable on delicate cycle in lukewarm water using mild soap (or neutral detergent, a mild detergent containing no alkalies or bleaches), with no bleach or fabric softener, and laid flat to dry; or it can be drycleaned. Falk has a gauge of 24 stitches per 4 inches (10cm) on size 3 (3.25mm) or 4 (3.5mm) needles. Each ball is 1¾ oz/50g/116 yards.

Smart is also a 4-ply combed yarn in 100% pure new wool. It is machine washable on delicate cycle in lukewarm water using mild soap (or neutral detergent), with no bleach or fabric softener, and laid flat to dry; or it can be drycleaned. Smart has a gauge of 22 stitches per 4 inches (10cm) on size 3 (3.25mm) or 4 (3.5mm) needles. Each ball is 1¾ oz/50g/110 yards.

Alfa is a soft, combed, chunky-weight yarn made of 85% pure new wool and 15% mohair. It is machine-washable on delicate cycle in lukewarm water using mild soap (or neutral detergent), with no bleach or fabric softener, and laid flat to dry; or it can be drycleaned. Alfa has a gauge of 13 stitches per 4 inches (10cm) on size 10½ (6.5mm) needles. Each ball is 1¾ oz/50g/65 yards.

SUBSTITUTING YARNS

At the beginning of every pattern I have listed the yarn I used. Because there are only two yarn weights used—Falk and Smart are worsted weight and Alfa is chunky—it's easy to substitute another yarn of the same weight. In other words, you can use any medium-weight yarn in place of the Falk or Smart, and any bulky-weight yarn in place of the Alfa. Also, if you have yarn leftover from one hat, you can easily use it for another hat. ✜

READING A YARN LABEL

Most yarn comes wrapped in a label that gives you lots of helpful information.

FIBER CONTENT: The label tells you what kind(s) of fiber the yarn is made from and, if it's a blend, in what proportion.

QUANTITY: The label will tell you the weight (in ounces and/or grams) and length (in yards and/or meters) of the yarn in the skein.

DYE LOT: Yarn is dyed in limited quantities at one time, and there can be minor variations between dye lots. So, if you need more than one skein, make sure you buy skeins of the same color yarn from one dye lot.

GAUGE AND NEEDLE SIZE: The gauge is the number of stitches and rows in a 4-inch square, using the recommended size needles. (More about gauge on page 47.)

CARE INSTRUCTIONS: The label explains how to wash items made from the yarn, usually in symbols. It's good to know how to care for the hat you are going to make.

NEEDLES AND OTHER TOOLS

Needles come in different types, materials, and sizes. Straight needles are used for knitting back and forth, circular needles—two needles joined by a thin cord—for knitting in the round, and double-pointed needles (DPNs) for small projects and for finishing off the top of the hats. There are also cable needles for holding stitches aside when you are knitting stitches out of order when you make cables. Needles come in a variety of materials: plastic, wood, and metal. Experiment with different types of needles in different materials to see what works best for you. The size of the needle refers to its thickness, usually given in both U.S. sizes and metric: for example, size 4 (3.5mm). The length of circular needles is measured from one point, along the cord, to the other point.

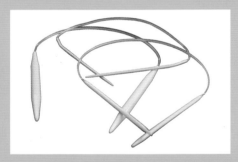

circular needles

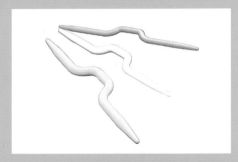

cable needles

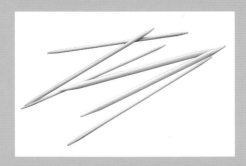

double-pointed needles

Needle-chaos can be very frustrating. You can make a needle organizer easily with a piece of wood: drill some holes in the top and nail it to the wall, with the holes pointing up. On the front, label the sizes of the needles you use.

Tapestry needles (or **yarn needles**) have blunt tips and large eyes and are used to weave in yarn ends when you have finished knitting.

Stitch markers help you keep track of where you are in the pattern. They can be simple plastic circles or fancy beaded rings.

A **row counter** helps you keep track of how many rows you have knitted.

Keep a small pair of **scissors** handy to cut the yarn and a **tape measure** to measure your knitting. A **crochet hook** is great for picking up a dropped stitch or for weaving in ends. And a **knitting bag** helps you keep your current project and the tools you need in one place. ✤

HOW TO READ THE PATTERNS

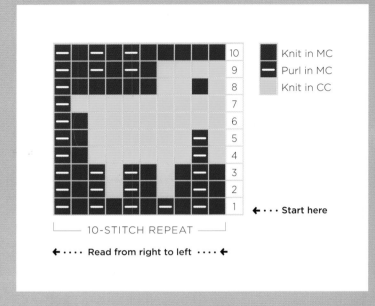

Knit in MC
Purl in MC
Knit in CC

←···· Start here

└─ 10-STITCH REPEAT ─┘

←···· **Read from right to left** ····←

This chart shows a pattern made of knit and purl stitches in two colors. See Klaus's hat on page 144.

ach pattern in this book starts with a list of the yarn and tools you'll need, the gauge (see opposite), the size of the hat, the pattern itself, and often a chart if there is a motif. (See below for more information on how to read the charts.) It's always best to read through the entire pattern before starting, to make sure you understand the directions and the stitches. (If not, check out "Help Desk" on page 156 for a refresher.)

In most of the hat directions, the top of the hat is shaped by asking you to decrease following my decrease formula on page 50. You may want to read that before starting, too.

Most patterns use more than one color yarn and these colors are indi-cated by MC for the main color and CC for the contrasting color. CC1 and CC2 are used if there are two con-trasting colors. If there are two more than three colors in the hat, then the yarns are listed as A, B, C, and D. Check out the knitting abbreviations (opposite) for a list of the more com-mon abbreviations used in pattern instructions.

READING CHARTS

Each chart in the book shows one motif only; you will repeat the motif all around the hat to create the design. (The number of motifs that will fit depends on how many stitches wide the motif is and how many stitches you cast on for your hat.)

Take a look at the sample chart above. Each square of a chart represents one stitch. You always read pattern charts *from right to left*. This is important; if there are letters in your chart, they will come out backwards if you work the other way. You always read the rows *from bottom to top*.

The color of each square tells you what color yarn to use for that stitch. And a symbol in the square (or lack thereof) tells you what kind of stitch to do. A key next to each chart shows you all the col-ors and stitches used in that motif.

TIP If the charts seem overwhelming and you'd rather try a pattern without a chart first, check out the hats on pages 68, 72, 86, 92, 112, 130, and 142.

KNITTING ABBREVIATIONS

Knitting patterns use a standard set of abbreviations. Once you become familiar with them, you'll be able to read any knitting pattern. Here are the basic abbreviations used in this book.

* *	repeat steps between asterisks as many times as indicated
beg	beginning
BO	bind off
C	cable
CC	contrast color
cn	cable needle
CO	cast on
DPN	double-pointed needle
k	knit
k2tog	knit 2 stitches together (decrease)
kfb	knit into front and back of same stitch (increase)
LH	left-hand
m1	make 1 stitch (increase)
MC	main color
p	purl
p2tog	purl 2 stitches together (decrease)
pm	place marker
RH	right-hand
sl1	slip 1 stitch
St st	stockinette stitch
St(s)	stitch(es)
yo	yarn over

GAUGE

Your knitting gauge is how many stitches per inch of knitted fabric you produce with a given needle size. You measure this by knitting a swatch—a sample square of knitting made before you start your hat— and then counting how many stitches you have in 4 inches. This is important because if your gauge is looser than called for, your hat will be too big. If it is tighter than called for, you may end up with a hat that's too small.

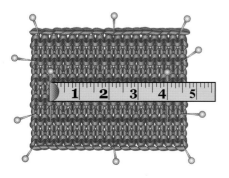

To measure your gauge:

• Knit a sample swatch, about 5 inches square, using the yarn from your project and the needle size called for in the pattern.

• Without stretching the swatch, place it flat on an ironing board and pin the edges.

• With a ruler, count the number of stitches in a 4-inch section. You may want to measure this in different places just to be sure.

• Refer to the pattern gauge. If your gauge is tighter (more stitches per inch than called for), use a larger needle size and swatch again. If your gauge is looser (fewer stitches per inch than called for), use a smaller needle size and swatch again. Continue to make swatches until you have knit in the gauge called for in the pattern. ❖

HAT SIZE

Each of the fifty hats in this book was designed and made in one of three sizes: small, medium, or large. Most of the hats are medium, with a few smalls and a handful of larges. One way to start a hat in this book is just to choose your favorite design and then make it for someone that size. Another way is to measure (or estimate) the head circumference of your hat recipient, find the correct size using the chart opposite, and then choose a hat in that size. Most young children and some teens will take a small; most women will take medium; and many men will take a large. But this will vary depending on how some people like their hats to fit.

ICON	SIZE	FITS THIS HEAD CIRCUMFERENCE	PATTERNS ON THESE PAGES
S	Small	17 ¾ – 19 inches (45 – 48cm)	62, 76, 104, 130
M	Medium	19 – 21¼ inches (48 – 54cm)	54, 60, 64, 66, 68, 70, 72, 74, 78, 80, 82, 84, 88, 92, 96, 98, 100, 102, 108, 110, 112, 116, 120, 122, 124, 126, 128, 134, 136, 138, 140, 142, 144, 146, 148, 150
L	Large	21¼ inches – 22 ¾ inches (54 – 58cm)	56, 58, 86, 90, 94, 106, 114, 118, 132, 152

ADJUSTING THE SIZE

What if you want to make one of the 50 hats, but it isn't in the right size? The motifs that repeat around most of the hats make it difficult to adjust their sizes greatly, but here are a few suggestions.

For smaller size adjustments, you can try adding or subtracting stitches to make the circumference larger or smaller. My general rule of thumb for an adult hat is to cast on approximately 90 stitches with the Falk and Smart yarns, and 60 stitches with the Alfa yarn. It is no problem to increase the number of stitches up to approximately 100, or to 65 respectively. (The numbers will vary slightly according to the number of stitches in the repeating motif.) In most cases, at least when you knit for an adult, this will work fine. I do, however, deviate upward and downward from this number when I knit hats for people who deviate quite a lot in head size (like children), or when a knitting technique makes the hat tighter than it would have been with normal knitting. For example, Anfinn (page 86) has a big head, and the technique of having columns of alternating colors around the hat makes it a lot less stretchy. So for Anfinn's hat, I cast on 110 stitches.

Keep in mind that the added or subtracted stitches will affect the hat's design. If there is a chart, it may be best to just add or subtract a stitch or two between repeats of the motif.

A knit hat stretches, so it can be comfortable on a number of different head sizes, but if you are unable to pull it down over your ears, it can be very irritating. If you want to make the hat larger, just knit another 4 to 6 rows before you start decreasing. ✤

KNITKID'S DECREASING FORMULA

If you want the top of your hat to look nice, you must decrease properly. On most of my hats, I decrease at six constant points, which creates a spiral effect on top of the hat. To make it easy, I use a basic formula that tells me exactly where in each round to make a decrease. This formula is used in almost every pattern in the book.

Decreasing evenly at six points creates an attractive spiral at the top of the hat.

The decreasing formula is: the number of stitches minus twelve divided by six equals the number of stitches between each decrease, or

$$\frac{\text{number of stitches} - 12}{6} = \begin{array}{l}\text{number of}\\\text{stitches}\\\text{between}\\\text{each}\\\text{decrease}\end{array}$$

Let's say the hat has 90 stitches:

90 − 12 = 78
78 / 6 = 13

This means that for the first decrease row, you work 13 stitches normally, then decrease 1 stitch (k2tog). Work another 13 stitches, then decrease another stitch (k2tog). And so on, to the end of the round. Okay, then what?

To shape the crown nicely, you will decrease on every other round for 6 to 8 rounds. On each decrease round, you subtract 1 more from the number you calculated in the formula, above, to get the number of stitches between decreases. So, in this example, when you start your second decrease round you would work only 12 stitches between each decrease. On your third decrease round, you'd work only 11 stitches between decreases. Get the idea? When you have worked a couple of rounds with decreasing, you will see where to decrease.

After you've worked 6 to 8 rounds with decreasing on each second round, start decreasing on every round until you have only 6 stitches remaining on your needles. As your hat gets smaller, you'll eventually have to switch to double-pointed needles (DPNs).

It doesn't take a scholar to master the Knitkid decreasing formula; it just requires some patience—to read through the directions and to practice with yarn and needles in hand.

TIP While you're decreasing, it often helps to put the hat on your head, or preferably on the owner's head, to see if further adjustments are needed.

Here is the decreasing sequence in pattern language:

- Calculate the number of stitches (x) using the formula above.

- Round 1: *K2tog, work x stitches in pattern,* repeating between *s to end of round.

- Round 2: Work even in pattern, with no decreasing.

- Round 3: *K2tog, work (x − 1) stitches in pattern,* repeating between *s to end of round.

- Round 4: Work even in pattern, with no decreasing.

- Round 5: *K2tog, work (x − 2) stitches in pattern,* repeating between *s to end of round.

- Round 6: Work even in pattern, with no decreasing.

- Round 7: *K2tog, work (x − 3) stitches in pattern,* repeating between *s to end of round.

- Round 8: *K2tog, work (x − 4) stitches in pattern,* repeating between *s to end of round.

- Continue decreasing every round until only 6 stitches remain on your needle. ✧

TIP Need more help? If you're new to knitting or just feeling rusty, go to the Help Desk chapter on page 156 for instructions on all the knitting stitches and techniques used in this book.

HELGE

At one time the only things in Helge's life were school and soccer. He was in the somewhat unfortunate position of being too good for amateur teams, but not quite good enough for professional teams. That meant he practiced every day, but still had to hold down a regular job, too. His big hero is Eric Cantona, a muscular French player who played for Manchester United and was known for giving a karate kick to anyone in the stands who annoyed him. Cantona wore the number seven on his jersey, which explains the hat I designed for Helge. ✠

NEEDLES AND YARN

- Size 1 (2.5mm) 16-inch circular needle

- Size 4 (3.5mm) 16-inch circular needle and set of 4 or 5 double-pointed needles

- Sandnes Smart Superwash [100% wool; 1¾ oz/50g/110 yds], 1 skein each in Royal Blue (5846)—MC, Chocolate Taupe (3082)—CC1, and White (1001)—CC2

GAUGE

22 stitches = 4 inches (10cm)

PATTERN

- With smaller needle and MC, cast on 90 stitches. Place marker and join to knit in the round, being careful not to twist work.

- Knit 6 rounds.

- Purl 1 round.

- Switch to larger needle. Knit 1 round in CC1.

- Work 10-stitch repeat of chart, rows 1 through 12, changing colors as shown.

- After completing chart, work in stockinette stitch (knit every round) for 2¾ more inches (7cm) or to desired length, continuing to alternate between 2 rounds of CC1 and 2 rounds of MC.

- Decrease according to formula on page 50, still alternating CC1 and MC stripes, until 6 stitches remain.

- Cut working yarn, leaving 8-inch (20cm) tail. Using yarn needle, thread tail through remaining stitches, pulling tight to close top of hat. Weave in ends to finish.

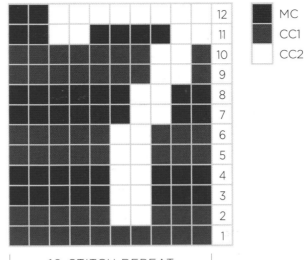

10-STITCH REPEAT

TORUNN grew up in a place a short ferry ride outside of Stavanger, in a rural area few city people have ever seen. To me, the fact that you have to cross a tiny part of the ocean to get there makes Torunn's childhood home quite exotic—which in turn makes Torunn quite exotic. Torunn is an occupational therapist, specializing in hands. In recent years, she has had her own hands full raising a beautiful daughter. Torunn is a nature person, and with this hat I tried to visualize how springtime brings nature back to life, just like nature in the springtime brings Torunn more to life.

NEEDLES AND YARN

- Size 1 (2.5mm) 16-inch circular needle

- Size 4 (3.5mm) 16-inch circular needle and set of 4 or 5 double-pointed needles

- Dale of Norway Falk yarn [100% wool; 1¾ oz/50g/116 yds], 1 skein each in Fern Green (9155)—MC and Natural (0020)—CC

GAUGE

24 stitches = 4 inches (10cm)

PATTERN

- With smaller needle and MC, cast on 96 stitches. Place marker and join to knit in the round, being careful not to twist work.

- Work 6 rounds of ribbing as follows: *knit 1, purl 1,* repeating between *s.

- Switch to larger needle. Knit one round.

- Work 8-stitch repeat of chart, rows 1 through 17, changing colors as shown.

- After completing chart, work in stockinette stitch (knit every round) with CC for 1½ more inches (4cm) or to desired length before starting decreases.

- Decrease according to formula on page 50 until 6 stitches remain.

- Cut working yarn, leaving 8-inch (20cm) tail. Using yarn needle, thread tail through remaining stitches, pulling tight to close top of hat. Weave in ends to finish.

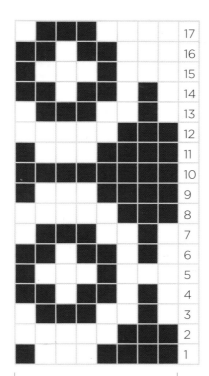

MC
CC

8-STITCH REPEAT

TORMOD loves newspapers and reads about ten a day, which means he keeps a lot of information about contemporary life in his head. There is probably also a tight schedule in his head. He is always in a hurry. Wherever he is, he is always on his way to someplace else, which is why you seldom see him without a jacket on. Tormod has moved a lot, having had many different jobs, but now he has settled in our town with his wife and two children. I hope he takes off his jacket at home. Tormod likes old political symbols, so I made him a hat with the old Soviet hammer and sickle. Politically he is not very red, though, so I made it yellow. ▓

NEEDLES AND YARN

- Size 1 (2.5mm) 16-inch circular needle
- Size 4 (3.5mm) 16-inch circular needle and set of 4 or 5 double-pointed needles
- Sandnes Smart Superwash [100% wool; 1¾ oz/50g/110 yds], 2 skeins in Dark Green (8681)—MC and 1 skein in Bright Yellow (2206)—CC

GAUGE

22 stitches = 4 inches (10cm)

PATTERN

- With smaller needle and MC, cast on 108 stitches. Place marker and join to knit in the round, being careful not to twist work.
- Knit 6 rounds.
- Purl 1 round.
- Switch to larger needle. Knit 1 round.
- Work 18-stitch repeat of chart, rows 1 through 14, changing colors as shown.
- After completing chart, work in stockinette stitch (knit every round) for 2½ more inches (6.5cm) or to desired length in MC before starting decreases.
- Decrease according to formula on page 50 until 6 stitches remain.
- Cut working yarn, leaving 8-inch (20cm) tail. Using yarn needle, thread tail through remaining stitches, pulling tight to close top of hat. Weave in ends to finish.

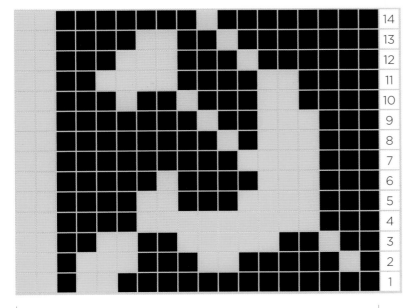

MC
CC

18-STITCH REPEAT

INGVILD M. lives what we all consider to be the good life with her husband and three children in a comfortable residential area in the center of southern Norway. When you enter their home, you immediately get the feeling that this is a laid-back, relaxed place. There is a lot of love in this house. All homes with children should probably be like this. Ingvild is an art teacher. She and her family love the mountains, and go skiing frequently. I made her a hat with white to match her smile, and orange to symbolize the sun. ✷

NEEDLES AND YARN

- Size 1 (2.5mm) 16-inch circular needle
- Size 4 (3.5mm) 16-inch circular needle and set of 4 or 5 double-pointed needles
- cable needle
- Dale of Norway Falk yarn [100% wool; 1¾ oz/50g/116 yds], 1 skein each in Natural (0020)—MC and Burnt Orange (3418)—CC

GAUGE

24 stitches = 4 inches (10cm)

PATTERN

- With smaller needle and MC, cast on 90 stitches. Place marker and join to knit in the round, being careful not to twist work.
- Work 7 rounds of ribbing as follows:
  knit 2, purl 1, repeating between *s.

- Switch to larger needle and attach CC. Work 1 round as follows: *Knit 2 with MC, purl 1 with CC,* repeating between *s to end of round.

- Work 3-stitch repeat of chart, maintaining colors and cabling as shown for 4¼ inches (10cm) from end of ribbing. The 2-stitch cross is formed as follows:
  2-stitch cross: *Place 1st stitch on cable needle (cn) and hold to back of work, knit next st, then knit st on cn.*

- Decrease according to formula on page 50, continuing *knit 2 with MC, purl 1 with CC* pattern until 6 stitches remain.

- Cut working yarn, leaving 8-inch (20cm) tail. Using yarn needle, thread tail through remaining stitches, pulling tight to close top of hat. Weave in ends to finish.

2
1

3-STITCH REPEAT

Knit in MC
2-stitch cross
Purl in CC

TOBIAS

The first time Tobias came to my apartment, he walked in very slowly, his eyes scanning the room almost without moving his head. After a while, he sat down and played quietly with some toys. While most children run around doing all kinds of unpredictable things, Tobias is more like a little philosopher, observing, thinking, and asking lots of questions. Of course, being a four-year-old boy, he is also capable of making quite a fuss, but to many busy parents a kid like Tobias would be a dream. Tobias loves farm machines in general, and tractors in particular, so I knit him a hat with tractors. ❖

NEEDLES AND YARN

- Size 1 (2.5mm) 16-inch circular needle

- Size 4 (3.5mm) 16-inch circular needle and set of 4 or 5 double-pointed needles

- Sandnes Smart Superwash [100% wool; 1¾ oz/50g/110 yds], 1 skein each in Royal Blue (5846)—MC, Medium Blue (5936)—CC1, and Cream/Winter White (1002)—CC2

GAUGE

22 stitches = 4 inches (10cm)

PATTERN

- With smaller needle and MC, cast on 84 stitches. Place marker and join to knit in the round, being careful not to twist work.

- Knit 6 rounds.

- Purl 1 round.

- Switch to CC1 and larger needle.

- Work 14-stitch repeat of chart, rows 1 through 12, changing colors as shown.

- After completing chart, work in stockinette stitch (knit every round) for 2¼ more inches (5.5cm) or to desired length, continuing to alternate between 2 rounds of CC1 and 2 rounds of MC.

- Decrease according to formula on page 50, still alternating between CC1 and MC, until 6 stitches remain.

- Cut working yarn, leaving 8-inch (20cm) tail. Using yarn needle, thread tail through remaining stitches, pulling tight to close top of hat. Weave in ends to finish.

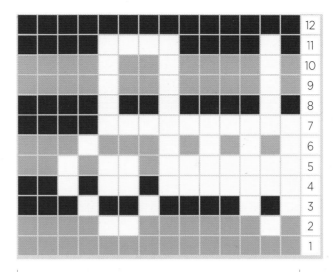

- MC
- CC1
- CC2

14-STITCH REPEAT

MOM

This is my mom and her name is Marit. She grew up in a tiny house on a farm with five siblings. The fact that a family of eight could live in such a small house is amazing. It must have been these intimate conditions that instilled in her the warm family values of a drill sergeant. My mom has not quite realized that her children are adults, have been adults for some years, and are supposed to stand on our own feet. But maybe this is the same for all mothers. Their children will always be their children. And maybe, despite our protests to the contrary, we want and need them to always be moms for us. ✤

NEEDLES AND YARN

- Size 1 (2.5mm) 16-inch circular needle

- Size 4 (3.5mm) 16-inch circular needle and set of 4 or 5 double-pointed needles

- Sandnes Smart Superwash [100% wool; 1¾ oz/50g/110 yds], 1 skein each in Bright Red (4109)—MC, Cream/Winter White (1002)—CC1, and Black (1099)—CC2

GAUGE

22 stitches = 4 inches (10cm)

PATTERN

- With smaller needle and MC, cast on 99 stitches. Place marker and join to knit in the round, being careful not to twist work.

- Knit 6 rounds.

- Purl 1 round.

- Switch to larger needle. Knit 1 round.

- Work 11-stitch repeat of chart, rows 1 through 7, changing colors as shown.

- After completing chart, knit 1 round in MC.

- Round 1: Switch to CC1. *K2tog, yo,* repeating between *s to end of round, (removing marker to complete last k2 tog, yo repeat. Replace marker. Note: Shifting the marker on round 1 creates the spiral stitch pattern.)

- Round 2: Switch to MC. Knit.

- Repeat Rounds 1 and 2 for 3¼ inches (8cm) or to desired length, ending with round 2.

- Knit 1 round with MC only, decreasing 3 stitches evenly over round. This produces an appropriate number of stitches (96) for the next step.

- Continuing with MC, decrease according to formula on page 50, until 6 stitches remain.

- Cut working yarn, leaving 8-inch (20cm) tail. Using yarn needle, thread tail through remaining stitches, pulling tight to close top of hat. Weave in ends to finish.

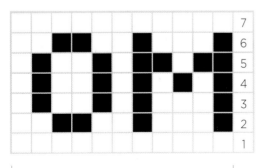

7
6
5
4
3
2
1

	CC1
■	CC2

—— 11-STITCH REPEAT ——

DAD This is my dad and his name is Sveinung. He spent most of his working life on oilrigs in the North Sea. Recently retired, he is now totally happy spending lazy days at home watching sports on television. He has a vivid imagination and lots of plans and ideas. Unfortunately, most of the plans tend to stay in his head.

One day he told me that he had solved the world's energy crisis. He had, in his head, created a power plant that would transform pressure at the bottom of the ocean into electricity. I told him to start drawing, but I guess the energy crisis will have to wait until there are no more games to watch on television. ✠

NEEDLES AND YARN

- Size 1 (2.5mm) 16-inch circular needle

- Size 4 (3.5mm) 16-inch circular needle and set of 4 or 5 double-pointed needles

- Sandnes Smart Superwash [100% wool; 1¾ oz/50g/110 yds], 2 skeins in Dark Moss Green (8764)—MC, and 1 skein each in Cream/Winter White (1002)—CC1, and Black (1099)—CC2

GAUGE

22 stitches = 4 inches (10cm)

PATTERN

- With smaller needle and MC, cast on 100 stitches in MC. Place marker and join to knit in the round, being careful not to twist work.

- Knit 6 rounds.

- Purl 1 round.

- Switch to larger needle. Knit 1 round.

- Work 10-stitch repeat of chart, rows 1 through 7, changing colors as shown.

- After completing chart, work in stockinette stitch (knit every round) with MC for 3½ more inches (9cm) or to desired length before starting decreases. Decrease 4 sts evenly over last round. This produces an appropriate number of stitches (96) for the next step.

- Decrease according to formula on page 50 until 6 stitches remain.

- Cut working yarn, leaving 8-inch (20cm) tail. Using yarn needle, thread tail through remaining stitches, pulling tight to close top of hat. Weave in ends to finish.

CC1

CC2

—— 10-STITCH REPEAT ——

RANDI

If the world were full of people like Randi, there would probably be peace everywhere and no poverty at all. Randi and her husband Tore (page 106) studied in Australia for several years, and have recently returned home to the cold north. From Down Under Randi brought back lots of ideas about how life should be, and is often critical of the Norwegian focus on career and material wealth. If it were up to Randi, we would all spend more time just singing and dancing. In Australia she was studying...singing and dancing. I made her a blue hat to match her eyes. ❖

NEEDLES AND YARN

- Size 8 (5mm) 16-inch circular needle
- Size 10½ (6.5mm) 16-inch circular needle and set of 4 or 5 double-pointed needles
- Sandnes Alfa [85% wool, 15% mohair; 1¾ oz/50g/65 yds], 2 skeins in Royal Blue (6863)—MC and 1 skein in Cream (1012)—CC

GAUGE

13 stitches = 4 inches (10cm)

PATTERN

- With smaller needle and MC, cast on 60 stitches. Place marker and join to knit in the round, being careful not to twist work.
- *Knit 1, purl 1,* repeating between *s to end of round.
- Attach CC. *Knit 1 with MC, knit 1 with CC,* repeating between *s to end of round.
- Work 6 rounds as follows: *Knit 1 with MC, purl 1 with CC,* repeating between *s.
- Switch to larger needle. Knit 1 round with MC.
- Next round (pattern round): *Yo, knit 4, k2tog, knit 4,* repeating between *s.
- Repeat pattern round until hat measures 6¼ inches (16cm) or to desired length from cast-on edge. Begin decreases as follows:
- Decrease round 1: *Knit 4, k2tog, knit 4,* repeating between *s to end of round.
- Next round: *Yo, knit 4, k2tog, knit 3,* repeating between *s to end of round.
- Decrease round 2: *Knit 4, k2tog, knit 3,* repeating between *s to end of round.
- Next round: *Yo, knit 4, k2tog, knit 2,* repeating between *s to end of round.
- Decrease round 3: *Knit 4, k2tog, knit 2,* repeating between *s to end of round.
- Decrease round 4: *Knit 4, k2tog, knit 1,* repeating between *s to end of round.
- Decrease round 5: *Knit 4, k2tog,* repeating between *s to end of round.
- Decrease round 6: *Knit 3, k2tog,* repeating between *s to end of round.
- Decrease round 7: *Knit 2, k2tog,* repeating between *s to end of round.
- Decrease round 8: *Knit 1, k2tog,* repeating between *s to end of round.
- Decrease round 9: *K2tog,* repeating between *s to end of round—6 stitches remaining.
- Cut working yarn, leaving 8-inch (20cm) tail. Using yarn needle, thread tail through remaining stitches, pulling tight to close top of hat. Weave in ends to finish.

ØYVIND

Give this man a book about a complicated topic, put him in a corner and leave him alone, and he is happy. Øyvind is a man of books, and like many book people, he has a beautiful, dry, smart sense of humor. When he's with people, Øyvind always sits there with his characteristic smile, right corner of his mouth pointing up and left corner pointing down, waiting for the right moment to pop out with a smart comment. Øyvind grew up in farm country but now lives in the city, so I knit him a hat with a cow's head design to remind him of his childhood home. ▦

NEEDLES AND YARN

- Size 1 (2.5mm) 16-inch circular needle
- Size 4 (3.5mm) 16-inch circular needle and set of 4 or 5 double-pointed needles
- Dale of Norway Falk yarn [100% wool; 1¾ oz/50g/116 yds], 1 skein each in Cocoa (3072)—MC, Burnt Orange (3418)—CC1, and Natural (0020)—CC2

GAUGE

24 stitches = 4 inches (10cm)

PATTERN

- With smaller needle and MC, cast on 90 stitches. Place marker and join to knit in the round, being careful not to twist work.
- Work 2 rounds of ribbing as follows:
  Knit 3, purl 3, repeating between *s.
- Switch to CC1. Knit 1 round.
- Work 2 more rounds of *knit 3, purl 3* ribbing, still using CC1.
- Switch to MC. Knit 1 round.
- Work 2 more rounds of *knit 3, purl 3* ribbing, still using MC.
- Switch to CC2 and larger needle.
- Work 11-stitch repeat of chart, rows 1 through 12, changing colors as shown.
- After completing chart, work in stockinette stitch (knit every round) for 2¾ more inches (7cm) or to desired length, continuing to alternate between 3 rounds of MC and 3 rounds of CC1.
- Decrease according to formula on page 50, still alternating colors, until 6 stitches remain.
- Cut working yarn, leaving 8-inch (20cm) tail. Using yarn needle, thread tail through remaining stitches, pulling tight to close top of hat. Weave in ends to finish.

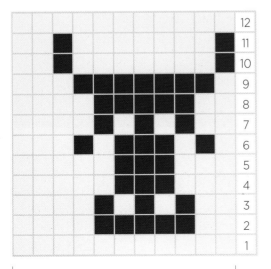

— 11-STITCH REPEAT —

 MC

CC2

ÅSE is my girlfriend and, of course, the cutest and nicest person in this book. She is a hero to me, a teacher in a school for special needs children. She is sort of a quiet person, and she never gets mad at me—or if she does, you can hardly tell. She grew up partly in the city of Bergen, and partly on a small island named Stord, which has given her the softest, mildest dialect. If you close your eyes when she is talking, it feels as if you are lying on a bed of fine silk. Åse has been an important source of technical support for my knitting, and, naturally she has a lot of Knitkid hats. I made her this hat in black to match her calmness, with three orange stripes to underline her strength, endurance, and patience. ❖

NEEDLES AND YARN

- Size 1 (2.5mm) 16-inch circular needle
- Size 4 (3.5mm) 16-inch circular needle and set of 4 or 5 double-pointed needles
- Dale of Norway Falk yarn [100% wool; 1¾ oz/50g/116 yds], 2 skeins in Black (0090)—MC and 1 skein in Burnt Orange (3418)—CC

GAUGE

24 stitches = 4 inches (10cm)

PATTERN

- With smaller needle, cast on 90 stitches in MC. Place marker and join to knit in the round, being careful not to twist work.
- Work 8 rounds of ribbing as follows:
  knit 5, purl 5, repeat between *s to end of round.
- Switch to larger needle.
- Round 1: Switch to CC. Knit 1 round.
- Round 2: Switch to MC. Knit 1 round.
- Rounds 3 and 4: Work *knit 5, purl 5* ribbing, continuing in MC.
- Repeat rounds 1 through 4 two more times. You will have 3 CC stripes.
- Work *knit 5, purl 5* ribbing in MC for 3¾ more inches (9.5cm) or to desired length. Then begin decreases as follows:
- Decrease round 1: *Knit 5, purl 1, p2tog, purl 2,* repeating between *s to end of round.
- Next round: *Knit 5, purl 4,* repeating between *s to end of round.
- Decrease round 2: *Knit 5, purl 1, p2tog, purl 1,* repeating between *s to end of round.
- Next round: *Knit 5, purl 3,* repeating between *s to end of round.
- Decrease round 3: *Knit 5, purl 1, p2tog,* repeating between *s to end of round.
- Next round: *Knit 5, purl 2,* repeating between *s to end of round.
- Decrease round 4: *Knit 5, p2tog,* repeating between *s to end of round.
- Next round: *Knit 5, purl 1,* repeating between *s to end of round.
- Decrease round 5: *Knit 4, k2tog,* repeat between *s to end of round.
- Decrease round 6: *Knit 3, k2tog,* repeat between *s to end of round.
- Decrease round 7: *Knit 2, k2tog,* repeat between *s to end of round.
- Decrease round 8: *Knit 1, k2tog,* repeat between *s to end of round.
- Decrease round 9: *K2tog,* repeat between *s to end of round.
- Cut working yarn, leaving 8-inch (20cm) tail. Using yarn needle, thread tail through remaining stitches, pulling tight to close top of hat. Weave in ends to finish.

EIRIK

If I could place Eirik in any historical setting, it would be in fifteenth-century French aristocracy. The way he moves, the way he speaks, his whole appearance is that of someone visiting from another time. I sometimes think he's just here gathering information about us, then planning to head back home in his time machine to give lectures about life in the twenty-first century. Eirik works in television and was the first person to bring the story of my knitting project to the television screen. His story was first shown locally, then nationally. He also made a 30-second video about me called "The world's fastest knitter," which you might find on YouTube. I think Eirik looks really good in brown, and the blue matches his eyes. ✦

NEEDLES AND YARN

- Size 1 (2.5mm) 16-inch circular needle
- Size 4 (3.5mm) 16-inch circular needle and set of 4 or 5 double-pointed needles
- Dale of Norway Falk yarn [100% wool; 1¾ oz/50g/116 yds], 2 skeins in Cocoa (3072)—MC and 1 skein each in Off-white (0017)—CC1 and Ocean Blue (6027)—CC2

GAUGE

24 stitches = 4 inches (10cm)

PATTERN

- With smaller needle and MC, cast on 90 stitches. Place marker and join to knit in the round, being careful not to twist work.
- Knit 6 rounds.
- Purl 1 round.
- Switch to larger needle. Knit 1 round.
- Work 9-stitch repeat of chart, rows 1 through 10, changing colors as shown.
- After completing chart, work in stockinette stitch (knit every round) for 3 more inches (7.5cm) or to desired length in MC before starting decreases.
- Decrease according to formula on page 50 until 6 stitches remain.
- Cut working yarn, leaving 8-inch (20cm) tail. Using yarn needle, thread tail through remaining stitches, pulling tight to close top of hat. Weave in ends to finish.

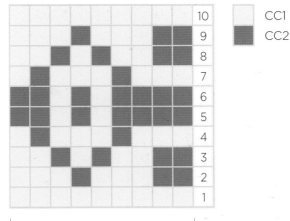

CC1
CC2

9-STITCH REPEAT

SARA

The first time I met Sara, she was scared of me, I think, because of my beard. If I came closer than ten feet, she would start screaming and hide behind her mother. Luckily, things have changed since then, and she even gets a bit excited when my girlfriend and I visit. Sara is not too fond of being in front of the camera, though. We had to spend a lot of time persuading her to let go of her mother's hand and be photographed. Seeing this portrait makes it all worthwhile. According to her parents, this little sweetheart is becoming quite smart and sly, so I designed her a hat with a small fox, the smartest little animal in the forest. ✳

NEEDLES AND YARN

- Size 1 (2.5mm) 16-inch circular needle

- Size 4 (3.5mm) 16-inch circular needle and set of 4 or 5 double-pointed needles

- Sandnes Smart Superwash [100% wool; 1¾ oz/50g /110 yds], 1 skein in Chocolate Taupe (3082)—MC

- Dale of Norway Falk yarn [100% wool; 1¾ oz/50g/116 yds], 1 skein each in Fern Green (9155)—CC1 and Off-white (0017)—CC2

GAUGE

22 stitches = 4 inches (10cm)

PATTERN

- Using smaller needles and MC, cast on 88 stitches. Place marker and join to knit in the round, being careful not to twist work.

- Work 1 round of ribbing as follows: *knit 1, purl 1,* repeating between *s to end of round.

- Switch to CC1. Knit 1 round.

- Work 1 round of *knit 1, purl 1* ribbing.

- Switch to MC. Knit 1 round.

- Work 2 more rounds of *knit 1, purl 1* ribbing.

- Switch to larger needle.

- Begin working 11-stitch repeat of chart, rows 1 through 12, changing colors as shown.

- After completing chart, work in stockinette stitch (knit every round) for 2½ more inches (6.5cm) or to desired length, continuing to alternate between 2 rounds of CC1 and 2 rounds of MC. Decrease 4 sts evenly over next round. This produces an appropriate number of stitches (84) for the next step.

- Decrease according to formula on page 50, still alternating between CC1 and MC, until 6 stitches remain.

- Cut working yarn, leaving 8-inch (20cm) tail. Using yarn needle, thread tail through remaining stitches, pulling tight to close top of hat. Weave in ends to finish.

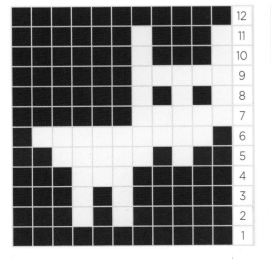

11-STITCH REPEAT

MC
CC1
CC2

STEINAR is a photographer, and a very passionate one.

On the day of the shoot for the photograph on pages 10–11, it was raining heavily, and Steinar was not dressed for the weather. I asked how he could concentrate, being so wet and cold. Sitting on his knees on the wet ground, he turned to me and said that he was so focused, he hadn't even noticed the rain. Steinar often wears off-white and beige sweaters and jackets, so I wanted to make him a hat that matched his clothing. The black circles are his camera lenses. ▦

NEEDLES AND YARN

- Size 1 (2.5mm) 16-inch circular needle

- Size 4 (3.5mm) 16-inch circular needle and set of 4 or 5 double-pointed needles

- Dale of Norway Falk yarn [100% wool; 1¾ oz/50g/116 yds], 1 skein each in Medium Sheep Heather (3841)—MC, Natural (0020)—CC1, and Black (0090)—CC2

GAUGE

24 stitches = 4 inches (10cm)

PATTERN

- With smaller needle and MC, cast on 90 stitches. Place marker and join to knit in the round, being careful not to twist work.

- Knit 6 rounds.

- Purl 1 round.

- Switch to larger needle and knit 1 round.

- Switch to CC1.

- Work 10-stitch repeat of chart, rows 1 through 10, changing colors as shown.

- After completing chart, work in stockinette stitch (knit every round) for 3 more inches (7.5cm), continuing to alternate between 2 rounds of MC and 2 rounds of CC1.

- Decrease according to formula on page 50, still alternating between MC and CC1, until 6 stitches remain.

- Cut working yarn, leaving 8-inch (20cm) tail. Using yarn needle, thread tail through remaining stitches, pulling tight to close top of hat. Weave in ends to finish.

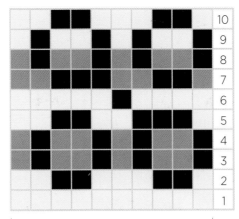

■	MC
■	CC1
■	CC2

10-STITCH REPEAT

INGRID ELIN

grew up in the south of Norway and, after several years in Oslo, she and her dog moved to Stavanger. She didn't know anyone here and was starting a new chapter in her life from scratch. I remember seeing her when I used to drive a bus. At that time I didn't know her at all. But I mean, look at her! A beauty like this doesn't go unnoticed getting on and off your bus. A couple of years later we ended up in the same social network. Now she and her boyfriend are friends with my girlfriend and me. She is a kick boxer and a very stylish woman, so she needed a hat with a bright color and simple horizontal lines. ⊞

NEEDLES AND YARN

- Size 1 (2.5mm) 16-inch circular needle
- Size 4 (3.5mm) 16-inch circular needle and set of 4 or 5 double-pointed needles
- Dale of Norway Falk yarn [100% wool; 1¾ oz/50g/116 yds], 2 skeins in Red (4018)—MC and 1 skein each in Off-white (0017)—CC1 and Black (0090)—CC2

GAUGE

24 stitches = 4 inches (10cm)

PATTERN

- With smaller needle and CC2, cast on 90 stitches. Change to MC and larger needle, place marker and join to knit in the round, being careful not to twist work.
- Work 10-stitch repeat of chart, rows 1 through 11, changing colors as shown.

- Repeat rounds 1 through 11 two more times, completing 3 black and white stripes.
- Continue in knit 5, purl 5 ribbing with MC only for ¾ more inches (2cm) or to desired length before starting decreases.
- Decrease as follows:
- Decrease round 1: *Knit 5, purl 1, p2tog, purl 2,* repeat between *s.
- Next round: *Knit 5, purl 4,* repeat between *s.
- Decrease round 2: *Knit 5, purl 1, p2tog, purl 1,* repeat between *s.
- Next round: *Knit 5, purl 3,* repeat between *s.
- Decrease round 3: *Knit 5, purl 1, p2tog,* repeat between *s.
- Next round: *Knit 5, purl 2,* repeat between *s.

- Decrease round 4: *Knit 5, p2tog,* repeat between *s.
- Next round: *Knit 5, purl 1,* repeat between *s.
- Decrease round 5: *Knit 4, k2tog,* repeat between *s.
- Decrease round 6: *Knit 3, k2tog,* repeat between *s.
- Decrease round 7: *Knit 2, k2tog,* repeat between *s.
- Decrease round 8: *Knit 1, k2tog,* repeat between *s.
- Decrease round 9: *K2tog,* repeat between *s.
- Cut working yarn, leaving 8-inch (20cm) tail. Using yarn needle, thread tail through remaining stitches, pulling tight to close top of hat. Weave in ends to finish.

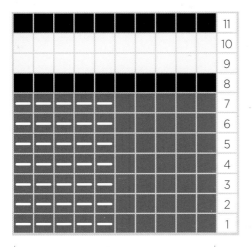

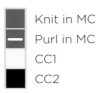

Knit in MC
Purl in MC
CC1
CC2

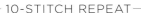
— 10-STITCH REPEAT —

TAGE Unlike some men, Tage has never been afraid of expressing his emotions. This has made him a big hit with the ladies at school. Once he was even observed bending down on one knee to propose. Combined with the fact that he is also very entertaining, both verbally and physically, it's easy to see why his nickname is "Mr. Popular." Recently he has started performing street dancing, and his moves are really impressive. I made him a hat with his nickname repeated all the way around, so you can see it from every direction. The bright blue plays up his intensely blue eyes, another reason he's so popular. ❖

NEEDLES AND YARN

- Size 1 (2.5mm) 16-inch circular needle
- Size 4 (3.5mm) 16-inch circular needle and set of 4 or 5 double-pointed needles
- Dale of Norway Falk yarn [100% wool; 1¾ oz/50g/116 yds], 1 skein each in Soft Blue (5943)—MC and Charcoal Heather (0083)—CC

GAUGE

24 stitches = 4 inches (10cm)

PATTERN

- With smaller needle and MC, cast on 96 stitches. Place marker and join to knit in the round, being careful not to twist work.
- Knit 6 rounds.
- Purl 1 round.
- Switch to larger needle. Knit 1 round.
- Work 16-stitch repeat of chart, rows 1 through 15, changing colors as shown.

- After completing chart, work in stockinette stitch (knit every round) for 2 more inches (5cm) or to desired length with MC before starting decreases.
- Decrease according to formula on page 50 until 6 stitches remain.
- Cut working yarn, leaving 8-inch (20cm) tail. Using yarn needle, thread tail through remaining stitches, pulling tight to close top of hat. Weave in ends to finish.

MC
CC

16-STITCH REPEAT

VENKE used to be a model, and there is no reason why she should not still be one. She now runs her own graphic design business, makes digital art, and sometimes sings for a local artist who produces electronic music. She is also interested in fashion and collecting old furniture. Venke is always very enthusiastic, but she can be a little absentminded. She often seems to lose track of her belongings, especially her keys. She is a fragile beauty, so a butterfly seemed appropriate for her hat. ✤

NEEDLES AND YARN

- Size 1 (2.5mm) 16-inch circular needle

- Size 4 (3.5mm) 16-inch circular needle and set of 4 or 5 double-pointed needles

- Dale of Norway Falk yarn [100% wool; 1¾ oz/50g/116 yds], 2 skeins in Electric Blue (5646)—MC and 1 skein in Off-white (0017)—CC

GAUGE

24 stitches = 4 inches (10cm)

PATTERN

- With smaller needle, cast on 85 stitches in MC. Place marker and join to knit in the round, being careful not to twist work.

- Knit 6 rounds.

- Purl 1 round.

- Change to larger needle. Knit 1 round.

- Work 17-stitch repeat of chart, rows 1 through 12, changing colors as shown.

- After completing chart, work in stockinette stitch (knit every round) with MC for 2 more inches (5cm) or to desired length before starting decreases. On last row, knit to last 2 stitches, k2tog. This produces an appropriate number of stitches (84) for the next step.)

- Decrease according to formula on page 50 until 6 stitches remain.

- Cut working yarn, leaving 8-inch (20cm) tail. Using yarn needle, thread tail through remaining stitches, pulling tight to close top of hat. Weave in ends to finish.

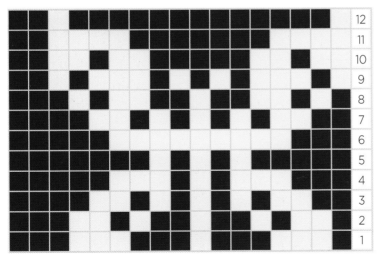

17-STITCH REPEAT

■ MC
□ CC

ANFINN and I have a common interest: kiteboarding. Kiteboarding involves standing on a board attached to a huge kite, which fills with air to propel you across water, land, or snow. Kiteboarding is not without its dangers. Both Anfinn and I are relatively new to the sport, still learning to master the art of steering the kite while at the same time balancing on the board. While I am nervous about the forces generated by the kite, Anfinn treats both the wind and kite fearlessly and totally without respect. When it comes to kiteboarding, my goal is to become as bold and fearless as this man. I made Anfinn a hat that matches his nice green eyes. I think the shape of his face is very classical and strong, so I put strong, decisive lines on his hat. ✜

NEEDLES AND YARN

- Size 1 (2.5mm) 16-inch circular needle
- Size 4 (3.5mm) 16-inch circular needle and set of 4 or 5 double-pointed needles
- Dale of Norway Falk yarn [100% wool; 1¾ oz/50g/116 yds], 1 skein each in Fern Green (9155)—MC and Black (0090)—CC1 and several yards in Off-white (0017)—CC2

GAUGE

24 stitches = 4 inches (10cm)

PATTERN

- With smaller needle and MC, cast on 100 stitches. Place marker and join to knit in the round, being careful not to twist work.
- Knit 1 round.
- Attach CC1. *Knit 5 in MC, knit 5 in CC1,* repeating between *s to end of round.
- Work 6 rounds as follows: *purl 5 in CC1, knit 5 in MC,* repeating between *s.
- Switch to larger needle. Knit 1 round in MC.
- Attach CC2. Knit 1 round in CC2.
- Switch to MC. Knit 1 round.
- Work as follows for 3½ inches (9cm) or to desired length before decreases: *Knit 5 in MC, knit 5 in CC1,* repeating between *s. Then begin decreases as follows:
- Decrease round 1: *Using MC: knit 1, k2tog, knit 2. Knit 5 in CC1, knit 5 in MC, knit 5 in CC1,* repeating between *s to end of round.
- Next round: *Knit 4 in MC, knit 5 in CC1, knit 5 in MC, knit 5 in CC1,* repeating between *s to end of round.
- Decrease round 2: *Knit 4 in MC. Using CC1: knit 1, k2tog, knit 2. Knit 5 in MC, knit 5 in CC1,* repeating between *s to end of round.
- Next round: *Knit 4 in MC, knit 4 in CC1, knit 5 in MC, knit 5 in CC1,* repeating between *s to end of round.
- Decrease round 3: *Knit 4 in MC, knit 4 in CC1. Using MC: knit 1, k2tog, knit 2. Knit 5 in CC1,* repeating between *s to end of round.
- Next round: *Knit 4 in MC, knit 4 in CC1, knit 4 in MC, knit 4 in CC1, knit 5 in MC,* repeating between *s to end of round.
- Decrease round 4: *Knit 4 in MC, knit 4 in CC1, knit 4 in MC, knit 4 in CC1. Using MC: knit 1, k2 tog, knit 2,* repeating between *s to end of round.
- Next round: *Knit 4 in MC, knit 4 in CC1, knit 4 in MC, knit 4 in CC1, knit 4 in CC1,* repeating between *s to end of round.
- Continue decreasing in this pattern on every round, reducing 1 stitch in every fourth color block and moving to the next color block on each round, until 8 stitches remain.
- Cut working yarn, leaving 8-inch (20cm) tail. Using yarn needle, thread tail through remaining stitches, pulling tight to close top of hat. Weave in ends to finish.

KATRIN has both brains and beauty. She is only seven years old and already trilingual. She speaks the Filipino Ilongo dialect, Norwegian, and some English, which she picked up from watching Barbie DVDs and singing along to Britney Spears. Katrin loves dressing up as a princess, and often wears her tiara from breakfast to bedtime. One would think that being a princess all day would be hard work, but Katrin never gets tired. She thinks going to bed is the most boring thing in the world, while staying outside to play with friends is much more appropriate. Oh, and of course, that all the boys in first grade are stupid. With such smarts and energy, Katrin is destined to become a successful New York business woman, so I gave her a hat with the Manhattan skyline. 🏵

NEEDLES AND YARN

- Size 1 (2.5mm) 16-inch circular needle

- Size 4 (3.5mm) 16-inch circular needle and set of 4 or 5 double-pointed needles

- Dale of Norway Falk yarn [100% wool; 1¾ oz/50g/116 yds], 1 skein each in Fuchsia/Peony (4516)—MC and Black (0090)—CC

GAUGE

24 stitches = 4 inches (10cm)

PATTERN

- With smaller needle and CC, cast on 90 stitches. Place marker and join to knit in the round, being careful not to twist work.

- Knit 6 rounds.

- Purl 1 round.

- Switch to larger needle. Knit 1 round.

- Work 5-stitch repeat of chart, rows 1 through 9, changing colors as shown.

- After completing chart, work in stockinette (knit every round) with MC for 3 inches (7.5cm) or to desired length before starting decreases.

- Decrease according to formula on page 50 until 6 stitches remain.

- Cut working yarn, leaving 8-inch (20cm) tail. Using yarn needle, thread tail through remaining stitches, pulling tight to close top of hat. Weave in ends to finish.

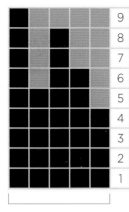

5-STITCH REPEAT

■ MC
■ CC

OLAV often gets comments about his name, Olav Larsen, because it is about as Norwegian as a name can be. Olav is a country-western musician and he always walks around town with his guitar. At some point he started a band that was gaining momentum, and I went to hear them play. Not only was the band really good, but Olav performed his own songs with the self-confidence, sadness, and sorrow of a real Texas cowboy. Way to go, Olav! I wanted to make Olav a hat that combined his African heritage with his life in Norway: orange for the hot climate in Africa, with the eight-leaf rose, which is a traditional Norwegian knitting motif. ✤

NEEDLES AND YARN

- Size 1 (2.5mm) 16-inch circular needle
- Size 4 (3.5mm) 16-inch circular needle and set of 4 or 5 double-pointed needles
- Dale of Norway Falk yarn [100% wool; 1¾ oz/50g/116 yds], 1 skein each in Burnt Orange (3418)—MC and Off-white (0017)—CC2
- Sandnes Smart Superwash [100% wool; 1¾ oz/50g/110 yds], 1 skein in Chocolate Taupe (3082)—CC1

GAUGE

Smart: 22 stitches = 4 inches (10cm)
Falk: 24 stitches = 4 inches (10cm)

PATTERN

- With smaller needle and MC, cast on 100 stitches. Place marker and join to knit in the round, being careful not to twist work.
- Knit 6 rounds.
- Purl 1 round.
- Switch to larger needle. Knit 2 rounds.
- Switch to CC1. Begin working 10-stitch repeat of chart, rows 1 through 9, changing colors as shown.
- After completing chart, work in stockinette stitch (knit every round) for 3 more inches (7.5cm) or to desired length, continuing to alternate between 2 rounds of MC and 2 of CC1. On last round, decrease 4 sts evenly over round. This produces an appropriate number of stitches (96) for the next step.
- Decrease according to formula on page 50, still alternating between colors, until 6 stitches remain.
- Cut working yarn, leaving 8-inch (20cm) tail. Using yarn needle, thread tail through remaining stitches, pulling tight to close top of hat. Weave in ends to finish.

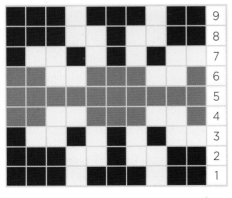

MC
CC1
CC2

10-STITCH REPEAT

KJERSTI is married to Øyvind (page 70). Together with their daughters Ingeborg (page 104) and Sara (page 76), they are the cutest family in Stavanger. Kjersti is known for being highly empathetic. She cries at sentimental movies, she cries at weddings, and she even cries when someone tells her a touching story. Kjersti also loves moving at high speed on skis, both on snow and water. She is also a very talkative, friendly person, and with the spirals on this hat I tried to capture her vivid, enthusiastic personality. The beige and black go perfectly with her coloring. ✣

NEEDLES AND YARN

- Size 8 (5mm) 16-inch circular needle and set of 4 or 5 double-pointed needles
- Sandnes Alfa [85% wool, 15% mohair; 1¾ oz/50g/65 yds], 2 skeins in Tan (2542)—MC and several yards in Black (1099)—CC

GAUGE

13 stitches = 4 inches (10cm)

PATTERN

- Cast on 59 stitches with CC. Place marker and join to knit in the round, being careful not to twist work.
- Switch to MC. Knit 1 round.
- Pattern round 1: *Knit 5, purl 5,* repeating between *s until 4 stitches remain. Purl 4. Remove marker, purl 1, replace marker.
- Repeat round 1 until hat measures 6 inches (15cm) or to desired length from cast-on edge. A spiral motif should emerge as the hat grows. In the last stitch of the last round, increase 1 stitch. This produces an appropriate number of stitches (60) for the next step.
- Begin decreases as follows:
- Decrease round 1: *Knit 5, purl 1, p2tog, purl 2,* repeating between *s to end of round.
- Next round: *Knit 5, purl 4,* repeating between *s to end of round.
- Decrease round 2: *Knit 5, purl 1, p2tog, purl 1,* repeating between *s to end of round.
- Next round: *Knit 5, purl 3,* repeating between *s to end of round.
- Decrease round 3: *Knit 5, purl 1, p2tog,* repeating between *s to end of round.
- Next round: *Knit 5, purl 2,* repeating between *s to end of round.
- Decrease round 4: *Knit 5, p2tog,* repeating between *s to end of round.
- Next round: *Knit 5, purl 1,* repeating between *s to end of round.
- Decrease round 5: *Knit 4, k2tog,* repeat between *s to end of round.
- Decrease round 6: *Knit 3, k2tog,* repeat between *s to end of round.
- Decrease round 7: *Knit 2, k2tog,* repeat between *s to end of round.
- Decrease round 8: *Knit 1, k2tog,* repeat between *s to end of round.
- Decrease round 9: *K2tog,* repeat between *s to end of round.
- Cut working yarn, leaving 8-inch (20cm) tail. Using yarn needle, thread tail through remaining stitches, pulling tight to close top of hat. Weave in ends to finish.

BÅRD is from the northernmost part of Norway, and that means that he is very down to earth, not very urban, and includes swear words in every sentence. Like his fellow northern Norwegians, he is also a storyteller. He can fill an entire evening with crazy stories about hard drinking and hard living. Back in the 1970s he was a radical, long-haired, flower-power, hippie. I imagine he spent much time in his twenties and thirties sitting around a bonfire with an acoustic guitar, singing songs about the workingman. One remaining trace of this period are his perfectly round, John Lennon-style glasses, which inspired the circles on his hat. The gray color comes from his stylish moustache. ✣

NEEDLES AND YARN

- Size 1 (2.5mm) 16-inch circular needle

- Size 4 (3.5mm) 16-inch circular needle and set of 4 or 5 double-pointed needles

- Sandnes Smart Superwash [100% wool; 1¾ oz/50g/110 yds], 1 skein each in Light Grey Tweed (1052)—MC, Black (1099)—CC1, and Gold (2025)—CC2

GAUGE

22 stitches = 4 inches (10cm)

PATTERN

- With smaller needle and CC1, cast on 98 stitches. Place marker and join to knit in the round, being careful not to twist work.

- Work 6 rounds of ribbing as follows:
  knit 1, purl 1, repeating between *s.

- Switch to larger needle and work 14-stitch repeat of chart, rows 1 through 11, changing colors as shown.

- After completing chart, work in stockinette stitch (knit every round) with MC for 3 more inches (7.5cm) or to desired length before starting decreases. Decrease 2 stitches evenly in the last knitted row. This produces an appropriate number of stitches (96) for the next step.

- Decrease according to formula on page 50 until 6 stitches remain.

- Cut working yarn, leaving 8-inch (20cm) tail. Using yarn needle, thread tail through remaining stitches, pulling tight to close top of hat. Weave in ends to finish.

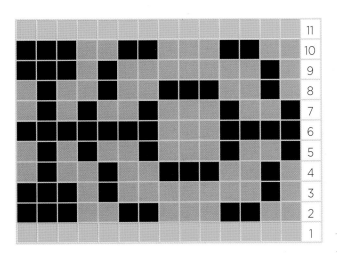

— 14-STITCH REPEAT —

MC
CC1
CC2

TONJE

You could say that this portrait is an example of art by accident. Tonje is a friend of my niece Sina, and she came along to Sina's photo shoot for fun. Tonje began digging through my pile of hats, trying on different ones. When she put on this one, it suited her so perfectly that we decided to include it. Tonje is a talented athlete, and plays handball and soccer.

Rumor has it, she's so good at soccer that sometimes she has to be taken off the field because the opposing team feels it is an unfair match. Maybe it's because fish move as swiftly and smoothly in water as Tonje does on the field, and the blue matches her intensely blue eyes, that the hat is a perfect match. ❖

NEEDLES AND YARN

- Size 1 (2.5mm) 16-inch circular needle

- Size 4 (3.5mm) 16-inch circular needle and set of 4 or 5 double-pointed needles

- Sandnes Smart Superwash [100% wool; 1¾ oz/50g/110 yds], 1 skein each in Royal Blue (5846)—MC, Chocolate Taupe (3082)—CC1, and White (1001)—CC2

GAUGE

22 stitches = 4 inches (10cm)

PATTERN

- With smaller needle and MC, cast on 96 stitches. Place marker and join to knit in the round, being careful not to twist work.

- Knit 6 rounds.

- Purl 1 round.

- Switch to larger needle.

- Work 12-stitch repeat of chart, rows 1 through 12, changing colors as shown.

- After completing chart, work in stockinette (knit every round) for 2¾ more inches (7cm) or to desired length, continuing to alternate between 2 rounds of MC and 2 rounds of CC1.

- Decrease according to formula on page 50, still alternating colors, until 6 stitches remain.

- Cut working yarn, leaving 8-inch (20cm) tail. Using yarn needle, thread tail through remaining stitches, pulling tight to close top of hat. Weave in ends to finish.

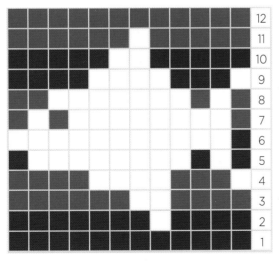

MC

CC1

CC2

12-STITCH REPEAT

STEIN In the early 1990s, I played guitar in a band that was enjoying some local success. We felt an international breakthrough was "just around the corner." Besides trying to make good music, we also tried to build a cool image. On the other side of town, Stein and his friends also had a band, but they had a different approach. They were more like an ironic band, making fun of the whole rock genre, and were very funny on stage. The irritating thing about Stein and his band is that they were way better musicians than we were. While we tried to be cool, they were cool—impressive musically and funny at the same time. Today Stein runs the annual Numusic festival in Stavanger. With this hat, I created a strong pattern to match Stein's somewhat severe look. ❖

NEEDLES AND YARN

- Size 8 (5mm) 16-inch circular needle
- Size 10½ (6.5mm) 16-inch circular needle and set of 4 or 5 double-pointed needles
- Sandnes Alfa [85% wool, 15% mohair; 1¾ oz/50g/65 yds], 1 skein each in Navy (5483)—MC, Brown (3082)—CC1, and Off-white (1002)—CC2

GAUGE

13 stitches = 4 inches (10cm)

PATTERN

- With smaller needle and MC, cast on 60 stitches. Place marker and join to knit in the round, being careful not to twist work.
- *Knit 1, purl 1,* repeating between *s to end of round.

- Switch to CC1. Knit 1 round.
- *Knit 1, purl 1,* repeating between *s to end of round.
- Switch back to MC. Knit 1 round.
- *Knit 1, purl 1,* repeating between *s to end of round.
- Switch to larger needle. Knit 1 round.
- Work 15-stitch repeat of chart, rows 1 through 13, changing colors as shown.
- After completing chart, work in stockinette stitch (knit every round) for 2 more inches (5cm) or to desired length, continuing to alternate between 2 rounds of MC and 2 rounds of CC1.
- Decrease according to formula on page 50, still alternating between colors, until 6 stitches remain.

- Cut working yarn, leaving 8-inch (20cm) tail. Using yarn needle, thread tail through remaining stitches, pulling tight to close top of hat. Weave in ends to finish.

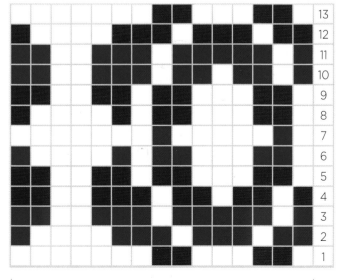

	MC
	CC1
	CC2

13
12
11
10
9
8
7
6
5
4
3
2
1

— 15-STITCH REPEAT —

RUKIA

I met Rukia while working a part-time job at a psychiatric hospital. Like me, she was an extra employee who was called only when additional help was needed. We did not talk very much, but I still decided I wanted to make this beautiful woman a hat, and include her in my book. I made a hat to match her dark hair, adding some orange elements to match her skin tone. I made a pattern that I imagined could be found on a traditional African instrument, like on a drum, to remind her of her African childhood. ⬦

NEEDLES AND YARN

- Size 1 (2.5mm) 16-inch circular needle
- Size 4 (3.5mm) 16-inch circular needle and set of 4 or 5 double-pointed needles
- Dale of Norway Falk yarn [100% wool; 1¾ oz/50g/116 yds], 2 skeins in Black (0090)—MC, and 1 skein each in Natural (0020)—CC1, and Burnt Orange (3418)—CC2

GAUGE

24 stitches = 4 inches (10cm)

PATTERN

- With smaller needle and MC, cast on 90 stitches. Place marker and join to knit in the round, being careful not to twist work.
- Work 6 rounds of ribbing as follows: *knit 1, purl 1,* repeating between *s.
- Switch to larger needle. Knit 1 round.
- Work 10-stitch repeat of chart, rows 1 through 13, changing colors as shown.
- After completing chart, work *knit 1, purl 1* pattern with MC for 2¾ inches (7cm) or to desired length before starting decreases.
- Decrease according to formula on page 50 until 6 stitches remain, maintaining ribbing where possible.
- Cut working yarn, leaving 8-inch (20cm) tail. Using yarn needle, thread tail through remaining stitches, pulling tight to close top of hat. Weave in ends to finish.

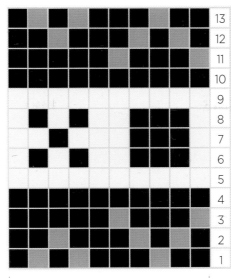

13
12
11
10
9
8
7
6
5
4
3
2
1

■ MC
□ CC1
▨ CC2

└─── 10-STITCH REPEAT ───┘

ATLE is one talented man. He studied mass media and now runs his own communications company. He also teaches art and design, and creates illustrations for books and magazines. Atle is interested in all things religious, philosophical, and theological, and is always reading books on these subjects. He is still very down to earth, though. He is also very environmentally conscious, fighting global warming by walking everywhere instead of driving. He walks more than any person I know, so putting footprints on his hat was only natural. ✤

NEEDLES AND YARN

- Size 1 (2.5mm) 16-inch circular needle
- Size 4 (3.5mm) 16-inch circular needle and set of 4 or 5 double-pointed needles
- Dale of Norway Falk yarn [100% wool; 1¾ oz/50g/116 yds], 2 skeins in Grey Heather (0007)—MC and 1 skein in Natural (0020)—CC

GAUGE

24 stitches = 4 inches (10cm)

PATTERN

- With smaller needle and MC, cast on 100 stitches. Place marker and join to knit in the round, being careful not to twist work.
- Knit 6 rounds.
- Purl 1 round.
- Switch to larger needle. Knit 1 round.
- Work 20-stitch repeat of chart, rows 1 through 17, changing colors as shown.
- After completing chart, work with MC in stockinette stitch (knit every round) for 1½ more inches (4cm) or to desired length before starting decreases.
- On last stockinette round, decrease 4 stitches evenly. This produces an appropriate number of stitches (96) for next step.
- Decrease according to formula on page 50 until 6 stitches remain.
- Cut working yarn, leaving 8-inch (20cm) tail. Using yarn needle, thread tail through remaining stitches, pulling tight to close top of hat. Weave in ends to finish.

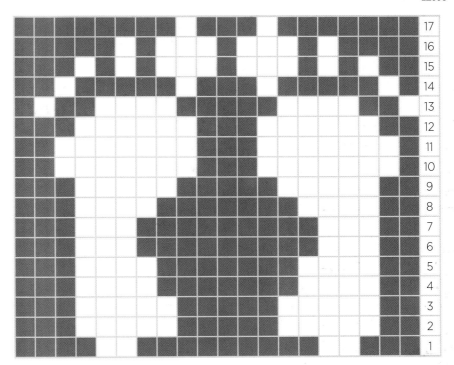

← 20-STITCH REPEAT →

 MC

CC

INGEBORG

The first time Ingeborg and I met, we became friends immediately. While my girlfriend Åse was talking with Ingeborg's parents about interest rates and other adult things, Ingeborg and I were on the floor competing to see who could do the craziest thing with our bodies, like standing on our head. Ingeborg and her sister, Sara (page 76), find it very hard to go to bed when they are told, so they have cultivated a large repertoire of tactics to delay bedtime. Unlike her little sister, Ingeborg doesn't have anything against being photographed. Being the sweetheart she is, Ingeborg got a pink hat with big hearts on it. ✤

NEEDLES AND YARN

- Size 8 (5mm) 16-inch circular needle

- Size 10½ (6.5mm) 16-inch circular needle and set of 4 or 5 double-pointed needles

- Sandnes Alfa Glitter [90% wool, 6.25% mohair, 3% acrylic, 0.75% polyester metallic; 1¾ oz/50g/66 yds], 1 skein each in Rose (4613)—MC, Dark Teal (6655)—CC1, and several yards in Black (1097)—CC2

GAUGE

13 stitches = 4 inches (10cm)

PATTERN

- With smaller needle and CC1, cast on 60 stitches. Place marker and join to knit in the round, being careful not to twist work.

- Knit 4 rounds.

- Purl 1 round.

- Switch to larger needle. Knit 1 round in CC2.

- Switch to MC and knit 1 round.

- Work 10-stitch repeat of chart, rows 1 through 8, changing colors as shown.

- After completing chart, work in stockinette stitch (knit every round) with MC for 2½ inches (6cm) more or to desired length before starting decreases.

- Decrease according to formula on page 50 until 6 stitches remain.

- Cut working yarn, leaving 8-inch (20cm) tail. Using yarn needle, thread tail through remaining stitches, pulling tight to close top of hat. Weave in ends to finish.

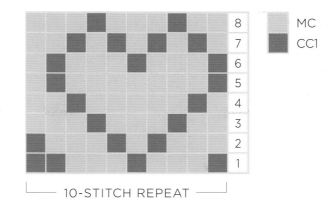

10-STITCH REPEAT

MC
CC1

TORE E.

Being with Tore is always entertaining. He and his wife Randi (page 68) recently returned from Australia, where they had lived for several years. That experience has led him to always ask critical questions about how we live our lives in the industrialized world. If it were up to Tore, life would be spent sitting on the beach with lots of red wine and all our friends gathered together. Tore is unusually sensitive and thoughtful, which sometimes affects his ability to get a good night's sleep. Still, he laughs a lot with a belly laugh that comes from deep inside, the kind that feels like it can lift off the roof. Given his laid-back philosophy, I simply had to make him a reggae-inspired hat, with bright colors and circles that are, yes, "joined together." ❖

NEEDLES AND YARN

- Size 1 (2.5mm) 16-inch circular needle
- Size 4 (3.5mm) 16-inch circular needle and set of 4 or 5 double-pointed needles
- Dale of Norway Falk yarn [100% wool; 1¾ oz/50g/116 yds], 1 skein each in Black (0090)—A, Poppy (3609)—B, Gold (2427)—C, and Burnt Orange (3418)—D

GAUGE

24 stitches = 4 inches (10cm)

PATTERN

- With smaller needle and A, cast on 100 stitches. Place marker and join to knit in the round, being careful not to twist work.
- Knit 6 rounds.
- Purl 1 round.
- Switch to larger circular needle. Knit 1 round.
- Work 20-stitch repeat of chart, rows 1 through 21, changing colors as shown.
- After completing chart, work 7 rounds of each color in stockinette in the sequence C, B, C, D and, *at the same time*, when 1½ inches (4cm) from last chart row, begin decreases.
- Decrease 4 sts evenly over next round. This produces an appropriate number of stitches (96) for the next step.
- Decrease according to formula on page 50 until 6 stitches remain.
- Cut working yarn, leaving 8-inch (20cm) tail. Using yarn needle, thread tail through remaining stitches, pulling tight to close top of hat. Weave in ends to finish.

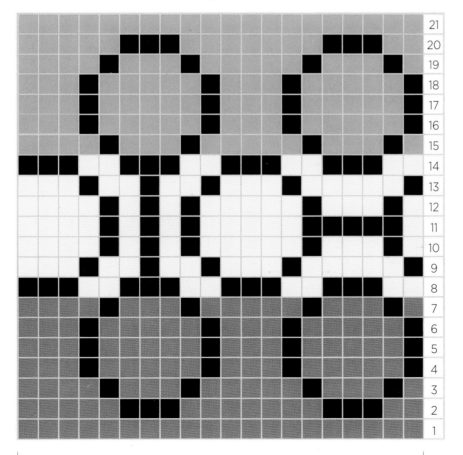

— 20-STITCH REPEAT —

■	A
▨	B
□	C
▤	D

KIRSTEN is my little sister and the smartest member of our family. She is the one we call when we have trouble programming the DVD player or figuring out the remotes. Kirsten also looks different from the rest of our family, with dark skin and long, black hair. Growing up, some of the neighbor kids thought she was adopted from a country far away. Now having successfully survived the first phase of raising three children, she is studying to become a teacher. She has what it takes to be a very good one, I think. Kirsten loves the color turquoise and, being my sister, I gave her a crown of flowers for her head. ✜

NEEDLES AND YARN

- Size 1 (2.5mm) 16-inch circular needle
- Size 4 (3.5mm) 16-inch circular needle and set of 4 or 5 double-pointed needles
- Dale of Norway Falk yarn [100% wool; 1¾ oz/50g/116 yds], 2 skeins in Turquoise (6415)—MC and 1 skein in Black (0090)—CC

GAUGE

24 stitches = 4 inches (10cm)

PATTERN

- With smaller needle and MC, cast on 100 stitches. Place marker and join to knit in the round, being careful not to twist work.

- Knit 6 rounds.

- Purl 1 round.

- Switch to larger needle. Knit 1 round.

- Work 10-stitch repeat of chart, rows 1 through 11, changing colors as shown.

- After completing chart, work in stockinette stitch (knit every round) with MC for 2¾ more inches (7cm) or to desired length before starting decreases. On last stockinette round, decrease 4 stitches evenly. This produces an appropriate number of stitches (96) for the next step.

- Decrease according to formula on page 50 until 6 stitches remain.

- Cut working yarn, leaving 8-inch (20cm) tail. Using yarn needle, thread tail through remaining stitches, pulling tight to close top of hat. Weave in ends to finish.

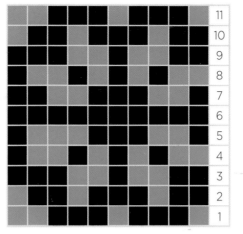

| | MC |
| | CC |

10-STITCH REPEAT

PER IVAR is a grounded, loyal, totally nice man who exudes good values. In the mid-1980s, military service brought him from a desolate area of Norway to our comparatively urban town, where he hooked up with some tough motorcycle kids. They toured Europe on their bikes, and that's when he caught the attention of my little sister. Now he is my brother-in-law. Per Ivar has been working with cars for most of his life and is currently employed by a BMW dealer. He specifically asked for a BMW hat, probably to impress his boss. ❖

NEEDLES AND YARN

- Size 1 (2.5mm) 16-inch circular needle

- Size 4 (3.5mm) 16-inch circular needle and set of 4 or 5 double-pointed needles

- Dale of Norway Falk yarn [100% wool; 1¾ oz/50g/116 yds], 2 skeins in Ocean Blue (6027)—MC, and 1 skein each in Off-white (0017)—CC1 and Black (0090)—CC2

GAUGE

24 stitches = 4 inches (10cm)

PATTERN

- With smaller needle and MC, cast on 90 stitches. Place marker and join to knit in the round, being careful not to twist work.

- Knit 6 rounds.

- Purl 1 round.

- Switch to larger needle. Knit 1 round.

- Work 30-stitch repeat of chart, rows 1 through 9, changing colors as shown.

- After completing chart, work in stockinette stitch (knit every round) with MC for 3½ more inches (9cm) before starting decreases.

- Decrease according to formula on page 50 until 6 stitches remain.

- Cut working yarn, leaving 8-inch (20cm) tail. Using yarn needle, thread tail through remaining stitches, pulling tight to close top of hat. Weave in ends to finish.

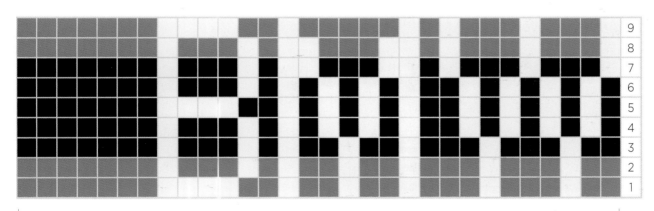

30-STITCH REPEAT

HEGE is the girlfriend of Per Kåre, one of my closest friends, which automatically upgrades Hege to the same position. Hege and Per Kåre live in a relatively new apartment complex, where Hege has shown a need for some improvement when it comes to organizing her closet. She has a lot of clothes, and they tend to end up in a big pile on their bedroom floor (at least, according to Per Kåre). Other than her closet issues, Hege is charming, warm-hearted, and cares about everyone around her. And with this hat, she becomes simply irresistible. The small red line at the bottom represents her passion for life, and the spirals represent her enthusiasm—as well as her disorganized closet. ❖

NEEDLES AND YARN

- Size 1 (2.5mm) 16-inch circular needle

- Size 4 (3.5mm) 16-inch circular needle and one set of 4 or 5 double-pointed needles

- Dale of Norway Falk yarn [100% wool; 1¾ oz/50g/116 yds], 1 skein each in Off-white (0017)—MC and Cocoa (3072)—CC1, and several yards of Red (4018)—CC2

GAUGE

24 stitches = 4 inches (10cm)

PATTERN

- With smaller needle and CC2, cast on 99 stitches. Place marker and join to knit in the round, being careful not to twist work.

- Attach MC and CC1. *Knit 5 with MC, purl 5 with CC1,* repeating between *s to last 4 stitches. Purl last 4 sts with CC1. Remove marker. Knit next stitch with CC1, replace marker.

- Switch to larger needle. Work 8 rounds as follows: *Knit 5 with MC, purl 4 with CC1, knit 1 with CC1,* repeating between *s to last 4 sts. Purl last 4 sts with CC1. Remove marker. Knit next stitch with CC1, replace marker. (Note: Shifting the marker one stitch to the left and knitting [not purling] the last stitch in CC1, forms a smooth spiral.)

- Switch to MC. Work 7 rounds in stockinette stitch (knit every round).

- *Knit 5 with MC, purl 5 with CC1,* repeating between *s to last 4 stitches. Purl last 4 sts with CC1. Remove marker. Knit next stitch with CC1, replace marker. Continue spiral pattern (knit 5 with MC, purl 4 with CC1, knit 1 with CC1) as above for 3½ inches (9cm) or to desired length before starting decreases. All decreases are done in the purl sections as follows:

- Decrease round 1: *Knit 5 with MC, then with CC1 purl 1, p2tog, purl 2,* repeating between *s to last 4 sts, purl 4 sts with CC1. Maintain colors as established.

- Next round: *Knit 5, purl 4,* repeating between *s to end of round.

- Decrease round 2: *Knit 5, purl 1, p2tog, purl 1,* repeating between *s to end of round.

- Next round: *Knit 5, purl 3,* repeating between *s to end of round.

- Decrease round 3: *Knit 5, purl 1, p2tog,* repeating between *s to end of round.

- Next round: *Knit 5, purl 2,* repeating between *s to end of round.

- Decrease round 4: *Knit 5, p2tog,* repeating between *s to end of round.

- Next round: *Knit 5, purl 1,* repeating between *s to end of round.

- Decrease round 5: *Continuing with MC only, knit 4, k2tog,* repeat between *s to end of round.

- Decrease round 6: *Knit 3, k2tog,* repeat between *s to end of round.

- Decrease round 7: *Knit 2, k2tog,* repeat between *s to end of round.

- Decrease round 8: *Knit 1, k2tog,* repeat between *s to end of round.

- Decrease round 9: *K2tog,* repeat between *s to end of round.

- Cut working yarn, leaving 8-inch (20cm) tail. Using yarn needle, thread tail through remaining stitches, pulling tight to close top of hat. Weave in ends to finish.

ØRJAN loves cycling off-road at full speed down steep hills. He bought himself a killer bicycle that looks strong enough to survive a nuclear attack and so expensive it must have cost several months' salary. He also loves skiing at high speed down snowy hills. In winter, Ørjan and I are ski pals, but with my Telemark skis, which are similar to cross-county skis, there is no way I can keep up with him. While I try making elegant curves to impress the women, Ørjan just wants to get down as quickly as possible and then hurry back up for the next ride. Just like a big kid. The circles on his hat are bicycle wheels. ✤

NEEDLES AND YARN

- Size 1 (2.5mm) 16-inch circular needle

- Size 4 (3.5mm) 16-inch circular needle and set of 4 or 5 double-pointed needles

- Sandnes Smart Superwash [100% wool; 1¾ oz/50g/110 yds], 1 skein each in Charcoal (1088)—MC and Cream (1012)—CC1, and several yards in Orange (2708)—CC2.

GAUGE

22 stitches = 4 inches (10cm)

PATTERN

- With smaller needle, cast on 98 stitches in MC. Place marker and join to knit in the round, being careful not to twist work.

- Knit 6 rounds.

- Purl 1 round.

- Switch to CC2 and larger needle. Knit 1 round.

- Switch to MC.

- Work 14-stitch repeat of chart, rows 1 through 18.

- After completing chart, switch to CC2. Knit 1 round.

- Work in stockinette stitch (knit every round) for 2 more inches (5cm) or to desired length in MC before starting decreases.

- Decrease according to formula on page 50 until 6 stitches remain.

- Cut working yarn, leaving 8-inch (20cm) tail. Using yarn needle, thread tail through remaining stitches, pulling tight to close top of hat. Weave in ends to finish.

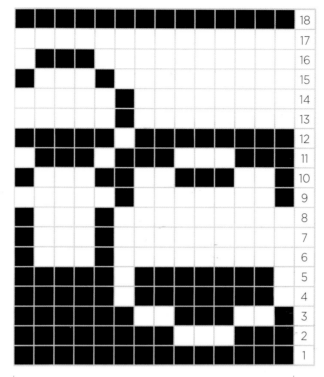

14-STITCH REPEAT

■ MC
□ CC1

SILJE and her husband recently moved from the big city of Oslo to our more modest town of Stavanger, a move that happened just in time, in my opinion. The move kept Silje from becoming way too urban and stylish for us. Sophisticated urban life is still quite evident in their kitchen, though. When Silje and her husband cook, they use ingredients that many in our town have never heard of. As Silje has been known to say, you will never find pre-mixed spices in her kitchen! She is a very down-to-earth person—smart, inclusive, and warm. With this hat I tried to convey the feel of a stylish piece of furniture, or the façade of an Art Deco building, to match her chic city image. ⊞

NEEDLES AND YARN

- Size 1 (2.5mm) 16-inch circular needle
- Size 4 (3.5mm) 16-inch circular needle and set of 4 or 5 double-pointed needles
- Sandnes Smart Superwash [100% wool; 1¾ oz/50g/110 yds], 2 skeins in Aqua (7033)—MC, and 1 skein in Wine (4065)—CC

GAUGE

22 stitches = 4 inches (10cm)

PATTERN

- With smaller needle and CC, cast on 96 stitches. Place marker and join to knit in the round, being careful not to twist work.
- Work 6 rounds of ribbing as follows: *knit 1, purl 1,* repeating between *s.
- Switch to larger needle. Knit 1 round.
- Work 8-stitch repeat of chart, rows 1 through 11, changing colors as shown.
- After completing chart, work stockinette stitch (knit every round) with MC for 3 more inches (7.5cm) before starting decreases.
- Decrease according to formula on page 50 until 6 stitches remain.
- Cut working yarn, leaving 8-inch (20cm) tail. Using yarn needle, thread tail through remaining stitches, pulling tight to close top of hat. Weave in ends to finish.

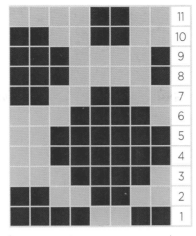

□ MC
■ CC

└ 8-STITCH REPEAT ┘

ARVID is a character like no other. He's happiest when he has time to be with his friends, and as long as he has an audience, he is entertained. He talks non-stop for hours. I imagine all the sentences lined up in his head, ready to be served. This flow of words only halts for a few short days each May due to a mild annual spring depression. Arvid has never cared much about education or a professional career, and he loves being politically incorrect. If everyone opposes a particular foreign policy, you can be certain that Arvid favors it. I made him a hat with waves because he works on an oilrig in the North Sea, and I used a clear blue to match both his eyes and the ocean. ▓

NEEDLES AND YARN

- Size 1 (2.5mm) 16-inch circular needle

- Size 4 (3.5mm) 16-inch circular needle and set of 4 or 5 double-pointed needles

- Dale of Norway Falk yarn [100% wool; 1¾ oz/50g/116 yds], 1 skein each in Off-white (0017)—MC, Electric Blue (5646)—CC1, and Black (0090)—CC2

GAUGE

24 stitches = 4 inches (10cm)

PATTERN

- With smaller needle and CC1, cast on 96 stitches. Place marker and join to knit in the round, being careful not to twist work.

- Work 2 rounds of ribbing as follows: *knit 2, purl 2,* repeating between *s.

- Switch to CC2. Knit 1 round.

- Work 2 more rounds of *knit 2, purl 2* ribbing, still using CC2.

- Switch to larger needle and work 6-stitch repeat of chart, rows 1 through 18, changing colors as shown.

- After completing chart, switch to MC and work in stockinette stitch (knit every round) for 2¼ more inches (5.5cm) or to desired length before starting decreases.

- Decrease according to formula on page 50 until 6 stitches remain.

- Cut working yarn, leaving 8-inch (20cm) tail. Using yarn needle, thread tail through remaining stitches, pulling tight to close top of hat. Weave in ends to finish.

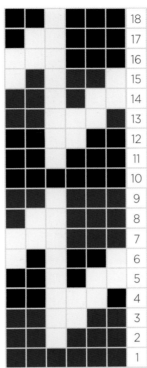

6-STITCH REPEAT

	MC
■	CC1
■	CC2

VU recently moved from the tropical and densely populated Ho Chi Minh City in Vietnam to the more desolate, cold world of Stavanger. Why he would want to do such a thing is an interesting question, and he sometimes talks with longing about big-city life in Vietnam. But each time he goes back to visit his hometown, he misses his new life on the cold Norwegian coast. Vu is a very positive person, always smiling. You seldom hear him say the word "no." He is studying Norwegian language and culture, preparing to start courses at the university. I made him a brown hat that complements his skin tones. ▓

NEEDLES AND YARN

- Size 1 (2.5mm) 16-inch circular needle
- Size 4 (3.5mm) 16-inch circular needle and set of 4 or 5 double-pointed needles
- cable needle
- Dale of Norway Falk yarn [100% wool; 1¾ oz/50g/116 yds], 2 skeins in Cocoa (3072)—MC and several yards in Natural (0020)—CC

GAUGE

24 stitches = 4 inches (10cm)

PATTERN

- With smaller needle and CC, cast on 90 stitches. Place marker and join to knit in the round, being careful not to twist work.
- Switch to MC. Knit 1 round.
- Work 6 rounds of ribbing as follows: *knit 3, purl 3,* repeating between *s.
- Switch to CC and larger needle. Knit 1 round.
- Switch to MC. Knit 1 round.
- Work 6-stitch repeat of chart, rows 1 through 12, with stitch patterns as shown. The two cables are formed as follows:
  Cross 4 front (left-leaning cable):
  Slip the next 3 stitches onto cable needle (cn) and hold to front of work, purl next stitch from left-hand needle, then knit the 3 sts from cn.

  Cross 4 back (right leaning cable):
  Slip the next stitch onto cn and hold to back of work, knit next 3 stitches from left-hand needle, then purl stitch from cn.

- When hat measures 6 inches (15cm) or desired length from cast-on edge, begin decreases.
- Decrease according to formula on page 50 , placing decreases in purl sections between cables for as long as possible. Continue in stockinette until 6 stitches remain.
- Cut working yarn, leaving 8-inch (20cm) tail. Using yarn needle, thread tail through remaining stitches, pulling tight to close top of hat. Weave in ends to finish.

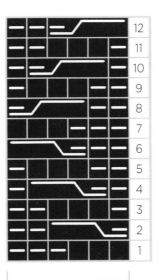

6-STITCH REPEAT

Knit

Purl

Cross 4 back

Cross 4 front

TONE is an outdoor junkie. If it were up to her, life would be spent outside. She spends summers on her surfboard, and winters on her skis. One might wonder, then, why she actually lives in the city. She admires those who crossed the Antarctic, climbed Mount Everest, or were guided somehow by their dreams. Tone is very sensitive; she's interested in the emotional processes that guide us, and the distinction between feelings and thoughts. If you say to Tone, "I feel that...," she will immediately stop you and ask, "Are you sure that is a feeling, and not a thought?" I made her a hat in red, the color of action, and in a vivid pattern that reflects her always-thoughtful self.

NEEDLES AND YARN

- Size 1 (2.5mm) 16-inch circular needle

- Size 4 (3.5mm) 16-inch circular needle and set of 4 or 5 double-pointed needles

- Sandnes Smart Superwash [100% wool; 1¾ oz/50g/110 yds], 1 skein each in Rust (3619)—MC, Cream (1012)—CC1, and Dark Tan (3161)—CC2

GAUGE

22 stitches = 4 inches (10cm)

PATTERN

- With smaller needle and MC, cast on 90 stitches. Place marker and join to knit in the round, being careful not to twist work.

- Work 8 rounds of ribbing as follows: *knit 3, purl 3,* repeating between *s.

- Switch to larger needle. Knit 1 round.

- Begin working 6-stitch repeat of chart, rows 1 through 6, changing colors as shown.

- When hat measures 5½ inches (14cm) or desired length from the cast-on edge, begin decreasing.

- Decrease according to formula on page 50, continuing to follow chart as far as possible as you decrease. Alternatively, ending with Row 6 of chart, drop CC1 and CC2 and knit only in MC as you decrease.

- When 6 stitches remain, cut working yarn, leaving 8-inch (20cm) tail. Using yarn needle, thread tail through remaining stitches, pulling tight to close top of hat. Weave in ends to finish.

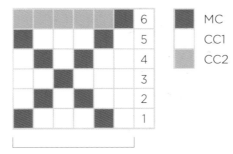

6-STITCH REPEAT

◼ MC
☐ CC1
▨ CC2

ODDVAR is the most optimistic person I know. He finds the positive side of any situation. While we were growing up, Oddvar was the leader without really knowing it. He set the tone for everything we did and all the things we found popular: American trucks, sailboats, music, and girls. After Oddvar got married, we didn't see him for ten years. Now that he's divorced, he is once again part of the gang, and both Oddvar and the gang are happy about that. Oddvar loves cars and engines. He recently dismantled, cleaned, fixed, and reassembled a Saab engine—an incredible achievement, if you ask me. This hat symbolizes the delicately moving parts of fine machinery. ❖

NEEDLES AND YARN

- Size 1 (2.5mm) 16-inch circular needle
- Size 4 (3.5mm) 16-inch circular needle and set of 4 or 5 double-pointed needles
- Sandnes Smart Superwash [100% wool; 1¾ oz/50g/110 yds], 2 skeins in Charcoal (1088)—MC and 1 skein in Cream/Winter White (1012)—CC

GAUGE

22 stitches = 4 inches (10cm)

PATTERN

- With smaller needle and MC, cast on 96 stitches. Place marker and join to knit in the round, being careful not to twist work.
- Knit 6 rounds.
- Purl 1 round.
- Switch to larger needle. Knit 1 round.
- Work 16-stitch repeat of chart, rows 1 through 15, changing colors as shown.

- When chart is completed, work in stockinette stitch (knit every round) with MC for 2¼ more inches (5.5cm) or to desired length before starting decreases.
- Decrease according to formula on page 50 until 6 stitches remain.
- Cut working yarn, leaving 8-inch (20cm) tail. Using yarn needle, thread tail through remaining stitches, pulling tight to close top of hat. Weave in ends to finish.

■ MC
□ CC

16-STITCH REPEAT

ASLAUG is my girlfriend's mother, and the fittest seventy-one-year-old woman I know. When she ties her shoes, she bends forward with straight legs like a teenager, ties her shoes, and then runs off—literally. When she is not out running, she is talking or reading. She loves information. When Åse and I visit, we sit for hours at the kitchen table. Åse and her mum just keep on talking…and talking…. My brain is not built for that much information, so I just sit and knit. After a weekend at Aslaug's place, I always return home with a lot of hats. Aslaug is very critical of modern life, but we are trying to show her that any self-respecting information junkie should at least get the Internet. I made her a hat that is full of information and energy, just like her. ✢

NEEDLES AND YARN

- Size 1 (2.5mm) 16-inch circular needle
- Size 4 (3.5mm) 16-inch circular needle and set of 4 or 5 double-pointed needles
- Sandnes Smart Superwash [100% wool; 1¾ oz/50g/110 yds], 1 skein each in Chocolate Taupe (3082)—MC, Moss (9544)—CC1, and White (1001)—CC2

GAUGE

22 stitches = 4 inches (10cm)

PATTERN

- With smaller needle and MC, cast on 96 stitches. Place marker and join to knit in the round, being careful not to twist work.
- Work 2 rounds of ribbing as follows: *knit 1, purl 1,* repeating between *s.
- Switch to CC1. Work 2 more rounds of ribbing.
- Switch to MC. Work 2 more rounds of ribbing.
- Switch back to CC1. Work 2 more rounds of ribbing (8 rounds of ribbing in total).
- Switch to MC and larger needle. Knit 1 round.
- Work 8-stitch repeat of chart, rows 1 through 17, using colors as shown.
- After completing chart, work in stockinette stitch (knit every round) for 1½ inches (3.5cm) or to desired length in stockinette, alternating between 2 rounds of CC1 and 2 rounds of MC.

- Decrease according to formula on page 50, still alternating colors, until 6 stitches remain.
- Cut working yarn, leaving 8-inch (20cm) tail. Using yarn needle, thread tail through remaining stitches, pulling tight to close top of hat. Weave in ends to finish.

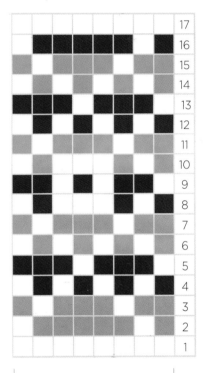

MC
CC1
CC2

8-STITCH REPEAT

TORE V. Tore is a man of hard science. Very hard. He is also a genius

with carpentry tools, measuring, hammering, sawing, and creating the most amazing constructions, such as his garage. A while ago, after completing many such projects, Tore took a much-needed break from carpentry. But as soon as our collective praise began to fade, he started hammering again, this time in his garden. Naturally, Tore's place soon became the natural spot for summer barbecues—and maybe also for aspiring architecture students. Recently seen wearing some hippie buttons, Tore now seems to be building a new image. By putting the international peace symbol on this green hat, I tried to give him a hand. ⧉

NEEDLES AND YARN

- Size 1 (2.5mm) 16-inch circular needle
- Size 4 (3.5mm) 16-inch circular needle and set of 4 or 5 double-pointed needles
- Dale of Norway Falk yarn [100% wool; 1¾ oz/50g/116 yds], 2 skeins in Fern Green (9155)—MC and 1 skein in Off-white (0017)—CC

GAUGE

24 stitches = 4 inches (10cm)

PATTERN

- With smaller needle and MC, cast on 90 stitches. Place marker and join to knit in the round, being careful not to twist work.
- Work 6 rounds of ribbing as follows: *knit 1, purl 1*, repeating between *s.
- Switch to larger needle. Knit 1 round.
- Work 15-stitch repeat of chart, rows 1 through 13, changing colors as shown.

- After completing chart, work in stockinette stitch (knit every round) with MC for 2½ more inches (6.5cm) or to desired length before starting decreases.
- Decrease according to formula on page 50 until 6 stitches remain.
- Cut working yarn, leaving 8-inch (20cm) tail. Using yarn needle, thread tail through remaining stitches, pulling tight to close top of hat. Weave in ends to finish.

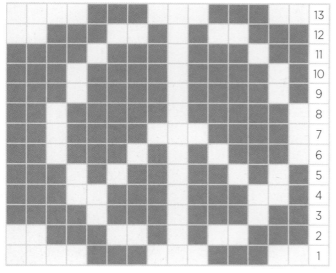

15-STITCH REPEAT

MC
CC

IDUN
The first time I met Idun, she was really shy. The second time, she was not shy at all. A few months ago, Idun managed to break one of her father's ribs. He was lying on the couch resting after work, and Idun was running around the room. She climbed onto the back of the couch, and before she knew it, she had fallen off the couch onto her father—knee first. This was when she learned that fathers are breakable. Idun's father was unable to laugh, sneeze, cough, or breathe deeply for weeks afterwards. I made her a blue hat to match her eyes, with a spiralling whirlwind-like design to match her whirlwind energy. ✤

NEEDLES AND YARN

- Size 1 (2.5mm) 16-inch circular needle

- Size 4 (3.5mm) 16-inch circular needle and set of 4 or 5 double-pointed needles

- Sandnes Smart Superwash [100% wool; 1¾ oz/50g/110 yds], 2 skeins in Royal Blue (5846)—MC and several yards in Cream/Winter White (1002)—CC

GAUGE

22 stitches = 4 inches (10cm)

PATTERN

- With smaller needle and MC, cast on 84 stitches. Place marker and join to knit in the round, being careful not to twist work.

- Knit 6 rounds.

- Purl 1 round.

- Attach CC and switch to larger needle. Knit 2 rounds in CC.

- Knit 1 round in MC.

- Next round (pattern round): *Yo, knit 5, k2tog, knit 5,* repeating between *s to end of round.

- Repeat pattern round until hat measures 5½ inches (14cm) or to desired length from cast-on edge. Begin decreases as follows:

  - Next round (Decrease round 1): *Yo, knit 5, k2tog, knit 5,* repeating between *s to end of round.

  - Decrease round 2: *Knit 5, k2tog, knit 5,* repeating between *s to end of round.

  - Repeat decrease rounds 1 and 2 two more times.

  - Repeat decrease round 2 until 6 stitches remain.

  - Cut working yarn, leaving 8-inch (20cm) tail. Using yarn needle, thread tail through remaining stitches, pulling tight to close top of hat. Weave in ends to finish.

MOSTAFA runs my favorite Turkish restaurant in Stavanger. The first time I went there, I was sitting at a table waiting to place my order when he came over, bent down slightly, resting his hands on the table, and looked deeply into my eyes. He stood like this for several seconds, making me feel like a kid who had done something terribly wrong. "You know what?" he finally asked. "If you start eating here, you will become a kebab addict. Here we make kebabs only with the finest ingredients, and they taste exactly like the kebabs you get in Turkey." And you know, he was right. The squares on his hat are tables at his restaurant. ❖

NEEDLES AND YARN

- Size 8 (5mm) 16-inch circular needle
- Size 10½ (6.5mm) 16-inch circular needle and set of 4 or 5 double-pointed needles
- Sandnes Alfa [85% wool, 15% mohair; 1¾ oz/50g/65 yds], 1 skein each in Black (1099)—MC, Heather Gray (1053)—CC1, and Off-white (1002)—CC2

GAUGE

13 stitches = 4 inches (10cm)

PATTERN

- With smaller needle and MC, cast on 64 stitches. Place marker and join to knit in the round, being careful not to twist work.
- Knit 6 rounds.
- Purl 1 round.
- Switch to larger needle. Knit 1 round.
- Attach CC1 and CC2. Work 8-stitch repeat of chart in stockinette, rows 1 through 13, changing colors as shown.
- After completing chart, work in stockinette stitch (knit every round) with MC for 2 more inches (5cm) or to desired length before starting decreases. In first round of stockinette section, increase two stitches evenly over the round. This produces an appropriate number of stitches (66) for the next step.
- Decrease according to formula on page 50 until 6 stitches remain.
- Cut working yarn, leaving 8-inch (20cm) tail. Using yarn needle, thread tail through remaining stitches, pulling tight to close top of hat. Weave in ends to finish.

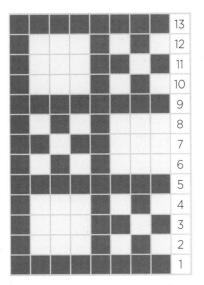

└ 8-STITCH REPEAT ┘

■ CC1
□ CC2

MARIA is a colorful person, both inside and out. She is probably the dandiest hairdresser in southern Norway. Together with a friend, she runs a salon that feels more suited to London or New York than the little town of Sandnes where she lives.

Maria has strong opinions, as well as a sharp, quick tongue; having discussions with her can be lots of fun because you have to keep on your toes. Maria loves to dress in bright colors, so for her hat, I used red for her passionate nature, and pink for her dandiness. ▓

NEEDLES AND YARN

- Size 1 (2.5mm) 16-inch circular needle
- Size 4 (3.5mm) 16-inch circular needle and set of 4 or 5 double-pointed needles
- Dale of Norway Falk yarn [100% wool; 1¾ oz/50g/116 yds], 1 skein each in Red (4018)—A, Pink (4415)—B, Black (0090)—C, and Off-white (0017)—D

GAUGE

24 stitches = 4 inches (10cm)

PATTERN

- With A and smaller needle, cast on 96 stitches. Place marker and join to knit in the round, being careful not to twist work.
- Work 8-stitch repeat of chart, rows 1 through 18, changing colors as shown.
- Repeat rounds 1-9 one more time, completing 3 black-and-white stripes.
- Work 5 rounds as follows: *Knit 4 in B, knit 4 in A,* repeating between *s.
- Work 5 rounds as follows: *Knit 4 in A, knit 4 in B,* repeat between *s.
- Work 5 rounds as follows: *Knit 4 in B, knit 4 in A,* repeating between *s.
- Begin decreasing as follows (Note: All decreases will occur in sections using Color B until these stitches are "used up".)
- Decrease round 1: *Knit 4 in A, knit 1 in B, k2tog in B, knit 1 in B,* repeating between *s to end of round.

- Next round: *Knit 4 in A, knit 3 in B,* repeating between *s to end of round.
- Decrease round 2: *Knit 4 in A, knit 1 in B, k2tog in B,* repeating between *s to end of round.
- Next round: *Knit 4 in A, knit 2 in B,* repeating between *s to end of round.
- Decrease round 3: *Knit 4 in A, k2tog in B,* repeating between *s to end of round.
- Next round: *Knit 4 in A, knit 1 in B,* repeating between *s to end of round.

- Decrease round 4: *Continuing with A only, knit 3, k2tog,* repeat between *s to end of round.
- Decrease round 5: *Knit 2, k2tog,* repeat between *s to end of round.
- Decrease round 6: *Knit 1, k2tog,* repeat between *s to end of round.
- Decrease round 7: *K2tog,* repeat between *s to end of round.
- Cut working yarn, leaving 8-inch (20cm) tail. Using yarn needle, thread tail through remaining stitches, pulling tight to close top of hat. Weave in ends to finish.

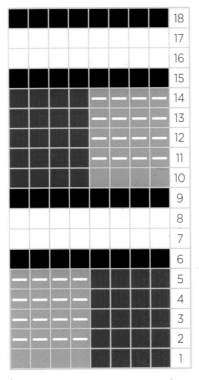

▓	A
▒	Knit in B
—	Purl in B
■	C
□	D

8-STITCH REPEAT

PER KÅRE is a graphic designer and his mind works in a very visual way. This may be why he almost never says more than one sentence at a time. Inside his head are almost exclusively logos in various states of completion. Even though Per Kåre was never the most verbal kid in school, he has a lot of life wisdom. He calls things as they really are, using few words in short sentences. Per Kåre has always been popular with women, probably because of his soft eyes and direct, no-nonsense way of talking. This logo-master considers the circle the most perfect geometric figure, so making him this hat was easy.

NEEDLES AND YARN

- Size 8 (5mm) 16-inch circular needle

- Size 10½ (6.5mm) 16-inch circular needle and set of 4 or 5 double-pointed needles

- Sandnes Alfa [85% wool, 15% mohair; 1¾ oz/50g/65 yds], 1 skein each in Brown (3082)—MC and Tan (2542)—CC

GAUGE

13 stitches = 4 inches (10cm)

PATTERN

- With smaller needle and MC, cast on 64 stitches. Place marker and join to knit in the round, being careful not to twist work.

- Attach CC. Work 6 rounds as follows: *Knit 1 in MC, purl 1 in CC,* repeating between *s.

- Switch to larger needle. Knit 1 round in MC.

- Work 8-stitch repeat of chart, rows 1 through 7, changing colors as shown.

- After completing chart, work in stockinette stitch (knit every round) with MC for 2½ more inches (6.5cm) or to desired length before starting decreases. In first round of stockinette section, increase two stitches evenly over the round. This produces an appropriate number of stitches (66) for the next step.

- Decrease according to formula on page 50 until 6 stitches remain.

- Cut working yarn, leaving 8-inch (20cm) tail. Using yarn needle, thread tail through remaining stitches, pulling tight to close top of hat. Weave in ends to finish.

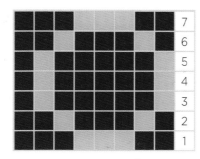

	MC
	CC

8-STITCH REPEAT

INGVILD A.

is a friend from way back, when we both lived in Oslo, the Norwegian capital. I was studying political science, and Ingvild was studying nightlife. She studied this subject quite intensively, only occasionally coming out during the day to say hello. After several years, the glow of nightlife lost its sparkle and she began working her way back to everyday life. She now spends her days photographing, painting, and raising two children. Ingvild is both strong and sweet, so I gave her a hat with an eagle that's pink. ❖

NEEDLES AND YARN

- Size 1 (2.5mm) 16-inch circular needle
- Size 4 (3.5mm) 16-inch circular needle and set of 4 or 5 double-pointed needles
- Dale of Norway Falk yarn [100% wool; 1¾ oz/50g/116 yds], 2 skeins in Dark Olive (8972)—MC and 1 skein in Blossom (4203)—CC

GAUGE

24 stitches = 4 inches (10cm)

PATTERN

- With smaller needle and MC, cast on 96 stitches. Place marker and join to knit in the round, being careful not to twist work.
- Knit 6 rounds.
- Purl 1 round.
- Switch to larger needle. Knit 1 round.
- Work 24-stitch repeat of chart, rows 1 through 20, changing colors as shown.

- After completing chart, work in stockinette stitch (knit every round) with MC for 2¼ more inches (5.5cm) or to desired length before starting decreases.
- Decrease according to formula on page 50 until 6 stitches remain.
- Cut working yarn, leaving 8-inch (20cm) tail. Using yarn needle, thread tail through remaining stitches, pulling tight to close top of hat. Weave in ends to finish.

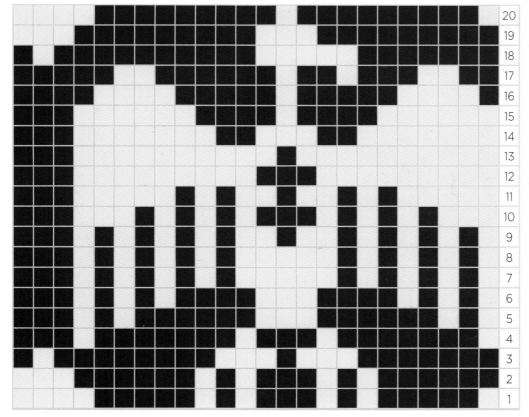

MC
CC

24-STITCH REPEAT

GULLEIV was the first...well, really the only one

of my friends to become a pop star. Gulleiv was only nineteen when he got a call from The September When, at the time a hot, up-and-coming band in Norway. Gulleiv was a hot, up-and-coming bass player, so it was a perfect fit. Suddenly he found himself standing before big crowds playing bass while looking at his muscles. He enjoyed each second of his new lifestyle, until one day it came crashing down. He then stopped being a pop star, started his own music studio, and began an aesthetic life of extreme exercise and exotic diets. The result is a mature and sensitive man full of experience, insight, and humor. I designed him—what else?—a hat covered in bass guitars. ✦

NEEDLES AND YARN

- Size 1 (2.5mm) 16-inch circular needle

- Size 4 (3.5mm) 16-inch circular needle and set of 4 or 5 double-pointed needles

- Dale of Norway Falk yarn [100% wool; 1¾ oz/50g/116 yds], 1 skein each in Cocoa (3072)—MC, Medium Sheep Heather (3841)—CC1, and Off-white (0017)—CC2

GAUGE

22 stitches = 4 inches (10cm)

PATTERN

- With smaller needle and MC, cast on 90 stitches. Place marker and join to knit in the round, being careful not to twist work.

- Knit 6 rounds.

- Purl 1 round.

- Switch to larger needle. Knit 1 round.

- Switch to CC1.

- Work 18-stitch repeat of chart, rows 1 through 21, changing colors as shown.

- After completing chart, work in stockinette stitch (knit every round) for 1½ more inches (4cm) or to desired length, continuing to alternate between 3 rounds of MC and 3 rounds of CC1.

- Decrease according to formula on page 50, continuing the alternating stripes, until 6 stitches remain.

- Cut working yarn, leaving 8-inch (20cm) tail. Using yarn needle, thread tail through remaining stitches, pulling tight to close top of hat. Weave in ends to finish.

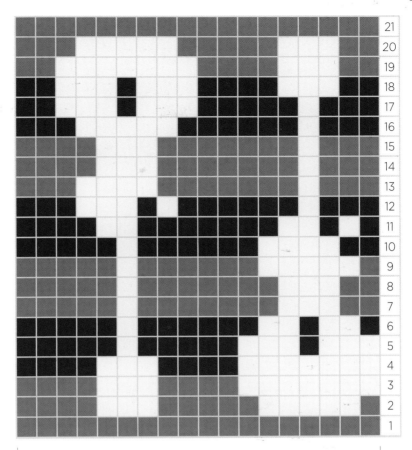

18-STITCH REPEAT

MC
CC1
CC2

DEBORAH

When Deborah and her family came to Norway from Sri Lanka in the 1970s, they were among the very first immigrants to our cold little corner of the world. It was only natural that they got some attention. Every time I see Debbi, she brings a big smile to my face.

She loves the city and is always dressed flawlessly, and I am quite sure that her closet is filled only with stylish, urban clothes. With her beautiful long hair, I knew that her hat had to be just the same black color, with a stripe of white and red to give it more life. ✽

NEEDLES AND YARN

- Size 1 (2.5mm) 16-inch circular needle

- Size 4 (3.5mm) 16-inch circular needle and set of 4 or 5 double-pointed needles

- Dale of Norway Falk yarn [100% wool; 1¾ oz/50g/116 yds], 2 skeins in Black (0090)—MC, and 1 skein each in Off-white (0017)—CC1, and Red (4018)—CC2

GAUGE

24 stitches = 4 inches (10cm)

PATTERN

- With smaller needle and MC, cast on 90 stitches. Place marker and join to knit in the round, being careful not to twist work.

- Knit 8 rounds as follows: *knit 1, purl 1,* repeating between *s to end of round.

- Switch to CC2 and larger needle. Knit 1 round.

- Switch to CC1. Knit 3 rounds.

- Switch to CC2. Knit 1 round.

- Switch to MC. Knit 1 round.

- Work *knit 1, purl 1* pattern, still using MC, for 3 inches (7.5cm) or to desired length.

- Decrease according to formula on page 50, maintaining ribbing where possible, until 6 stitches remain.

- Cut working yarn, leaving 8-inch (20cm) tail. Using yarn needle, thread tail through remaining stitches, pulling tight to close top of hat. Weave in ends to finish.

KLAUS is one of my closest friends, and the photographer for this book. A while back, Klaus and I began making electronic music together. We were very creative and productive, and suddenly we had a record deal. Soon we were on the road playing concerts in London, Stockholm, and other big cities. We called the band Elektrofant; you can still find the band logo on some of my hats. Besides being creative together, we also argued a lot. And I mean a lot! It is no secret among our friends that Klaus and I can argue at a high decibel. Klaus is a versatile person with many talents, and also a perfectionist in everything he does. Of course, I made him a hat with the Elektrofant band logo. ❖

NEEDLES AND YARN

- Size 1 (2.5mm) 16-inch circular needle

- Size 4 (3.5mm) 16-inch circular needle and set of 4 or 5 double-pointed needles

- Dale of Norway Falk yarn [100% wool; 1¾ oz/50g/116 yds], 2 skeins in Green Heather (7081)—MC and 1 skein in Dandelion (2417)—CC

GAUGE

24 stitches = 4 inches (10cm)

PATTERN

- With smaller needle and MC, cast on 90 stitches. Place marker and join to knit in the round, being careful not to twist work.

- Work 6 rounds as follows: *knit 1, purl 1,* repeating between *s.

- Switch to larger needle and work 1 more round of *knit 1, purl 1* ribbing.

- Work 10-stitch repeat of chart, rows 1 through 10, changing colors as shown. Note that all CC stitches are in stockinette (knit every stitch), while MC stitches continue to alternate in knit 1, purl 1 ribbing unless they fall directly above a CC stitch as shown in the chart.

- After completing chart, work *knit 1, purl 1* pattern with MC for 3½ inches (9cm) or to desired length before starting decreases.

- Decrease according to formula on page 50, maintaining ribbing where possible, until 6 stitches remain.

- Cut working yarn, leaving 8-inch (20cm) tail. Using yarn needle, thread tail through remaining stitches, pulling tight to close top of hat. Weave in ends to finish.

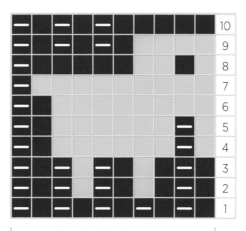

10-STITCH REPEAT

■ Knit in MC
▬ Purl in MC
▢ Knit in CC

TORGUNN is a nature freak.

She manages the local branch of the Norwegian Trekking Association, which means she is one of those lucky people who has somehow combined her hobby with her job. Not that hiking is her only hobby; she is active nonstop. Every day starts with a 6 AM workout, and each evening may include dinner at a fancy restaurant, a play, jazz concert, art exhibit, or a visit with her mother. Torgunn also happens to be expert at making people feel appreciated and valuable. I made her a hat that matches both her stylish black leather jacket, and her blonde hair. The red line symbolizes how the Norwegian Trekking Association marks the mountain routes with red paint on rocks so that their members don't get lost. ❖

NEEDLES AND YARN

- Size 1 (2.5mm) 16-inch circular needle
- Size 4 (3.5mm) 16-inch circular needle and set of 4 or 5 double-pointed needles
- Sandnes Smart Superwash [100% wool; 1¾ oz/50g/110 yds], 2 skeins in Cream (1012)—MC and 1 skein each in Burnt Orange (3619)—CC1 and Charcoal (1088)—CC2

GAUGE

22 stitches = 4 inches (10cm)

PATTERN

- With smaller needle and CC2, cast on 90 stitches. Place marker and join to knit in the round, being careful not to twist work.
- Work 7 rounds of ribbing as follows: *knit 3, purl 3,* repeating between *s.
- Switch to larger needle. Knit 1 round.
- Work 6-stitch repeat of chart, rows 1 through 12, changing colors as shown.
- After completing chart, work in stockinette stitch (knit every round) with MC for 2 inches (5cm) or to desired length before starting decreases.
- Decrease according to formula on page 50 until 6 stitches remain.
- Cut working yarn, leaving 8-inch (20cm) tail. Using yarn needle, thread tail through remaining stitches, pulling tight to close top of hat. Weave in ends to finish.

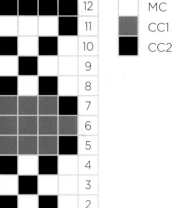

6-STITCH REPEAT

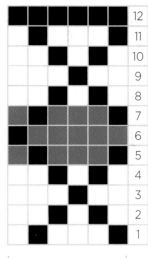

- MC
- CC1
- CC2

ANDREAS
has had the difficult task of growing up in a house full of women—strong women. His twin sisters and his mother have always known just how they wanted things to be, and Andreas has had to promote his masculine values and interests all by himself, and he has done it heroically, I think. How does he do this? By playing drums and listening to lots of rock 'n' roll. Since he dreams of success and fortune as a pop star, I gave him a hat with a wish for what lies ahead. ▩

NEEDLES AND YARN

- Size 1 (2.5mm) 16-inch circular needle
- Size 4 (3.5mm) 16-inch circular needle and set of 4 or 5 double-pointed needles
- Sandnes Smart Superwash [100% wool; 1¾ oz/50g /110 yds], 2 skeins in Cream (1012)—MC and 1 skein in Black (1099)—CC

GAUGE

22 stitches = 4 inches (10cm)

PATTERN

- With smaller needle and CC, cast on 90 stitches. Place marker and join to knit in the round, being careful not to twist work.
- Knit 6 rounds.
- Purl 1 round.
- Switch to MC and larger needle. Knit 1 round.
- Work 10-stitch repeat of chart, rows 1 through 11, changing colors as shown.
- After completing chart, work in stockinette stitch (knit every round) with MC for 3½ more inches (9cm) or to desired length before starting decreases.
- Decrease according to formula on page 50 until 6 stitches remain.
- Cut working yarn, leaving 8-inch (20cm) tail. Using yarn needle, thread tail through remaining stitches, pulling tight to close top of hat. Weave in ends to finish.

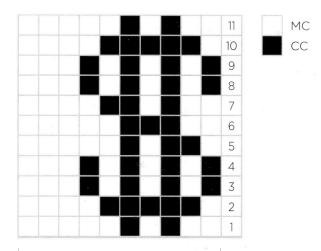

MC

CC

10-STITCH REPEAT

LINDA

is a walking stand-up comedy show. She is very observant, and everything she sees goes through some complex process in her head, eventually coming out in such a funny way that she brings down the house. She is the queen of one-liners. I think there are more things going on in her head than in most people's, and I imagine her brain is like a propeller, with a thousand things whirling around at any given moment. That's probably why she likes going out for a drink after work: she needs to cool down her mental motor. And that is why I knitted her a hat with wine glasses on it. ✤

NEEDLES AND YARN

- Size 1 (2.5mm) 16-inch circular needle
- Size 4 (3.5mm) 16-inch circular needle and set of 4 or 5 double-pointed needles
- Sandnes Smart Superwash [100% wool; 1¾ oz/50g/110 yds], 1 skein each in Wine (4065)—MC, Navy (5575)—CC1, and White (1001)—CC2

GAUGE

22 stitches = 4 inches (10cm)

PATTERN

- With smaller needle and MC, cast on 96 stitches. Place marker and join to knit in the round, being careful not to twist work.
- Knit 6 rounds.
- Purl 1 round.
- Switch to CC1 and larger needle.
- Work 16-stitch repeat of chart, rows 1 through 14, changing colors as shown.
- After completing chart, work in stockinette stitch (knit every round) for 3 more inches (7.5cm) or to desired length, continuing to alternate between 2 rounds of MC and 2 rounds of CC1.
- Decrease according to formula on page 50, still alternating between colors, until 6 stitches remain.
- Cut working yarn, leaving 8-inch (20cm) tail. Using yarn needle, thread tail through remaining stitches, pulling tight to close top of hat. Weave in ends to finish.

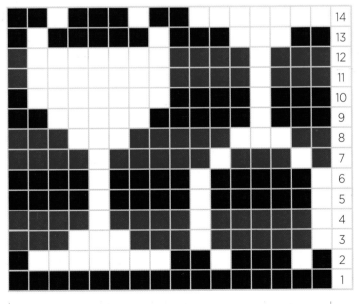

16-STITCH REPEAT

- MC
- CC1
- CC2

ARILD has a gift for making himself both seen and heard at social gatherings, no matter how large. Until quite recently, he was most frequently seen (and heard) at clubs and bars around town. After becoming a father, however, his life has become more centered on work and family. Arild runs an advertising and decoration company. In summer 2007, as a birthday gift to our queen, who was celebrating in Stavanger, he decorated our main square with a giant copy of Andy Warhol's famous portrait of her—created entirely out of flowers. To add to his already cool image, he drives a Jeep with really big wheels. I gave him a hat with a flower hidden in a camouflage design. If you look closely, you'll see it right above his eyes. ✤

NEEDLES AND YARN

- Size 1 (2.5mm) 16-inch circular needle

- Size 4 (3.5mm) 16-inch circular needle and set of 4 or 5 double-pointed needles

- Sandnes Smart Superwash [100% wool; 1¾ oz/50g/110 yds], 1 skein each in Gold (2025)—MC and Dark Green (8681)—CC

GAUGE

22 stitches = 4 inches (10cm)

PATTERN

- With smaller needle and CC, cast on 98 stitches. Place marker and join to knit in the round, being careful not to twist work.

- Knit 6 rounds.

- Purl 1 round.

- Switch to larger needle. Knit 1 round.

- Using MC and CC, work 6 rows in stockinette stitch (knit every round), changing color randomly every 1 to 5 stitches. (If this camouflage design feels too daunting, just knit the hat around the rose with MC.)

- On the next round, begin the 13-stitch chart, rows 1–11, changing colors as shown, then randomly knit 1 to 5 stitches, alternating between MC and CC to end of round (or continue in MC to end of round for solid version).

- After completing chart, continue working randomly with both colors (or with MC) until hat measures 5 inches (13cm) from cast-on edge. On last stockinette round, decrease 2 stitches evenly. This produces an appropriate number of stitches (96) for next step.

- Decrease according to formula on page 50 until 6 stitches remain. Cut working yarn, leaving 8-inch (20cm) tail. Using yarn needle, thread tail through remaining stitches, pulling tight to close top of hat. Weave in ends to finish.

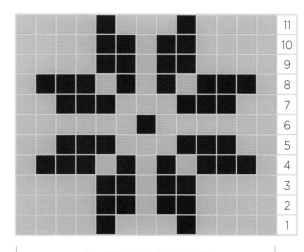

├──── 13-STITCH REPEAT ────┤

MC
CC

The chart above is for the rose in the center of the hat. The rest of the design is a randomly created pattern.

MORE HATS

Here are still more portraits of the 200 or so hats that I designed and knit for people over the past two years, all part of the Knitting Project. If you study these hats closely, with a pencil and a piece of graph paper in front of you, you will be able to sketch ideas for other designs to use to make more hats of your own. ✤

SECURITAS
Alarm
tilknyttet
SECURITAS-
SENTRAL

stiles
the TOOTHLESS
Tiger

THE BASICS

I f you're new to knitting, or haven't picked up needles in a while, it may be best to start with the basic stitches. Don't worry, knitting is actually easier than you think. Just spend some time practicing so your hands become familiar with the right moves. Once you have learned the basics, you'll be surprised at how easy it is to take knitting a step further.

If you already know how to knit, skip to the Basic Hat Pattern. I will guide you through three steps: a very simple hat pattern; then a hat with a design knitted in; and, finally, tips for creating your own designs.

BASIC STITCHES

The best way to learn how to knit is to actually try these stitches as you read about them, so before reading any further, gather the following materials:

* Size 10½ (6.5mm) 16-inch circular needle
* Some practice yarn

Casting on

"Casting on" means getting the first loops of yarn onto your needles.

1. Make a slipknot on one end of your needle. Be sure not to pull it too tightly. This counts as your first stitch. Make sure the tail end is approximately 40 inches (100cm) long.

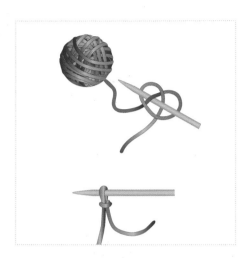

2. Hold that end of the needle with your right hand. Put your right index finger and thumb on the knot to keep it from slipping off the needle. Use your left hand to separate the two yarn tails over your index finger and your thumb respectively. Hold the two strands with the other fingers on your left hand.

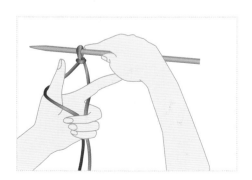

3. Bring the point of the needle down to pick up the yarn resting over your thumb, picking it up by going beneath the yarn and under it, and then pick up the yarn that is over your index finger.

4. Bring the loop of yarn from your thumb over and onto the needle, slipping it off your thumb. Now gently tug on both strands to tighten your loops slightly. Now you have your sec-

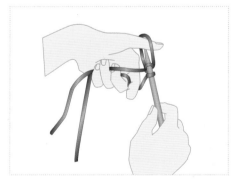

ond stitch.
5. Repeat steps 3 and 4 until you have cast on the number of stitches indicated in the pattern.

HOLDING YOUR NEEDLES

There are two ways to hold your needles: One is called American or English style where you hold the working yarn, the yarn that leads to the ball of yarn, in your right hand. The other is called Continental style where you hold the working yarn in your left hand. For both styles, you hold the needle with the cast-on stitches in your left hand and the empty needle (or the other end of your circular needle) in your right hand, with the working yarn extending out the back.

American or English style
Loop the working yarn over your *right* index finger. In this style of knitting you will use your right thumb and index finger to wrap the working yarn around the right hand needle.

Continental style
Loop the working yarn over your *left* index finger. In this style of knitting you will use the right needle to pick up the working yarn that is looped over your left finger.

Knit stitch (K)

The knit stitch is the mother of all stitches. It is the most common stitch, the one most patterns rely on. If you look at a knit stitch from the front of your work, it will look like a "V".

1. Put the tip of the right hand needle into the front loop of the first stitch on the left hand needle.

2. Bring the working yarn around the right-hand needle, going clockwise as shown.

3. Use the right needle to bring the new loop through the stitch, and push the stitch off the left hand needle. This is the hard part, and will take some practice before it feels natural for your fingers. Now you have got the first stitch on the second row (now resting on the right hand needle).

4. Repeat steps 1 through 3 all the way to the end of the row.

Purl stitch (P)

The purl stitch is the exact opposite of the knit stitch. If you look at a purl stitch from the front, it looks like a little bump. Knit stitches and purl stitches are really the same stitch, just on opposite sides. If you look at the back of a knit stitch, it will look like a purl.

1. Hold the needles the same way as you did for the knit stitch but bring the working yarn to the front of the needles. Put your right hand needle under the first stitch from right to left with right hand needle in front of the left hand needle. Bring the working yarn around the right needle from the front.

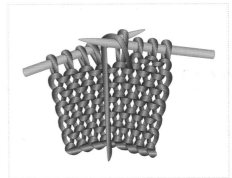

2. Bring the yarn through the loop, and then push the stitch off the left hand needle. You have now made the first purl stitch.

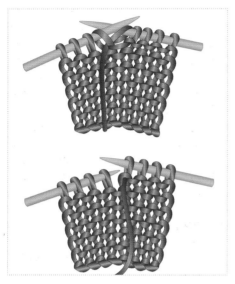

3. Repeat these 2 steps to make more purl stitches.

KNITTING IN THE ROUND

Knitting on circular needles, called knitting "in the round," is where you knit continuously building on the last round of stitches and end up with a tube shape (as opposed to knitting back and forth on straight needles where you end up with a flat piece of knitting that would have to be seamed to form a hat).

Cast on the number of stitches indicated in the pattern, making sure the stitches all face the same way, with the knots on the inside and the loops on the outside, and are not twisted around the needle. Slide a stitch marker onto your right-hand needle to indicate the beginning of the round; this is called "placing a marker." Each time you come back around to the marker, you will have completed another round and you'll just slide the marker from one needle to the other and keep going.

To join the work in a circle, knit the first stitch of the left-hand needle using the yarn coming from the last stitch on the right-hand needle.

INCREASING AND DECREASING

When you want to shape a piece of knitting, you need to "increase," or add stitches, and "decrease," or take away stitches. If you knit without decreasing you will end up with a long cylinder, not a hat.

The hard part about increasing and decreasing is not the stitches but rather figuring out where and how to increase or decrease. You need to do this correctly in order to shape the top of the hat; I have created a formula for this (see page 50). Once you know where to increase or decrease, here are the basic stitches to use.

FOR INCREASING:
Backwards loop cast-on

I use a very easy increase method in my hats. It is the same simple stitch used to cast on.

Make a loop with the working yarn on your thumb.

Pick up the front of the yarn with the right needle and then continue knitting. When you come to the next round, this loop will count as one extra stitch.

FOR DECREASING:
Knit 2 together (k2tog)

This is a simple decrease where you knit 2 stitches together as if they were one. Bring the right hand needle under both of the next 2 stitches, and then knit as you would a normal stitch, pushing them both off the left hand needle.

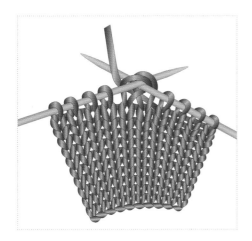

Purl 2 together (p2tog)

This is a simple decrease where you purl 2 stitches together as if they were one. Insert the top of the right hand needle into the front of both of the 2 next stitches, and then purl as you would a normal stitch, pushing them both off the left hand needle.

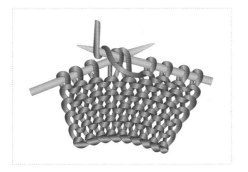

USING DOUBLE-POINTED NEEDLES

As you decrease the top of your hat to form the crown, you'll eventually have so few stitches that it will be impossible to keep using your circular needle. That's when you need to switch to double-pointed needles, or DPNs.

To change needles, take the first DPN in your right hand, and knit one third of the stitches onto on that needle. (You will have fewer stitches than shown here.) Then knit the next one-third onto the second DPN. Finally, knit the rest of the stitches onto the third DPN. Use a fourth DPN as your working needle.

FINISHING
Closing the top of the hat

After you have decreased to the point where you only have 10 stitches left, you have to close the top of the hat. First, cut the working yarn so you have a tail measuring about 8 inches (20cm). Thread this tail into a yarn needle and thread the tail through the 10 remaining stitches while they are still on the needle. Then remove the knitting needles. Thread the yarn tail through these stitches again, and pull the tail tightly to close up the top of the hat, and knot the tail. Weave the yarn tail into the fabric on the inside of the hat to hide the tail (see below).

Weaving in yarn ends

You need to weave in all yarn ends (from starting and finishing, color changes or ball changes) into the knitting.

Thread this tail into a yarn needle (or blunt tapestry needle), and bring the end under several bars of stitches on the wrong side, or inside, of the hat.

OTHER BASIC TECHNIQUES
Joining new yarn

When it comes time to change color, or when you need to attach a new ball of yarn because the old one has run out, just cut your working yarn at the beginning of a row, leaving a 6-inch-long (15cm) tail. There are two ways to attach the new yarn:

Tie the new color onto the old tail with a loose knot at the end of a row.

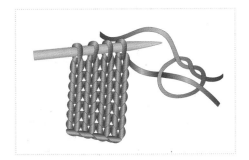

Start your next stitch, wrapping with both your old yarn tail and the new yarn, and pull both through. Then just drop your old yarn and continue knitting or purling as usual with your new yarn.

Yarn over (YO)

In some of my hats I have used this technique to make special lace-like patterns (see my mother's hat, for example, on page 64).

Bring the working yarn around to the front of your needle, then knit the next stitch.

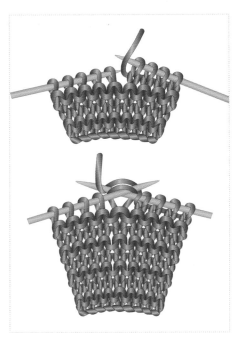

Stranding

When you knit with two colors at the same time, you keep the yarn not in use along the back of the knitting. The yarn you do not use will run along the back of the work.

Keep the yarn that runs on the back fairly loose. If the stranded yarn is pulled too tight it will make the hat pucker and the hat will not fit well.

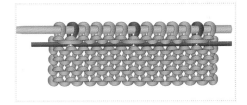

Cables

You have probably seen knit work that looks like it has a braid in it. In knitting we call this a cable, and it is created by knitting the stitches out of order.

1. Slip a number of stitches (the pattern you are knitting will tell you how many; here's it's 3) onto a cable needle or a double pointed needle.

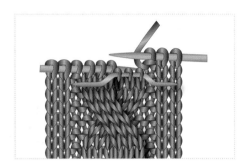

2. Bring these stitches in front of the work, as shown here, or behind the work (again, the pattern will tell you which way), and knit the next number of stitches (here 3) on the left needle.

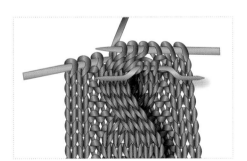

3. Knit the 3 stitches on the cable needle or DPN.

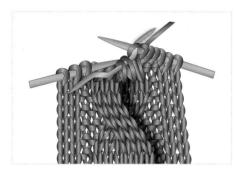

CABLING TRIAL RUN

Before you make a hat with cables, try one on a test swatch.

Cast on 19 stitches on a straight needle. Knit 6 rows, making knit stitches on the right side and purl stitches on the wrong side. Before you start cabling make sure that you are on the right side (knitting) of the work.

Knit the first stitch as normal. Now, slip the next 2 stitches onto a cable needle, and hold these stitches in the front of the work while knitting the next 2 stitches from the left-hand needle onto the right-hand needle. Now, knit the 2 stitches from the cable needle onto the right-hand needle. You can now see that cabling is merely stitches being crossed over one another.

Knit 1 stitch and then repeat the instructions above for cabling the next 4 stitches.

Continue in this way with 1 stitch separating every 4-stitch cable. When you have reached the end of the row, continue knitting (right side) and purling (wrong side) normally for 7 more rows. On every 8th row (right side) repeat the cabling instructions.

Cabling is a science all its own in knitting. Knitters can cable in a thousand different ways creating fantastic textural motifs. The basic technique, however, remains the same: stitches being moved back and forth, crossing over one another.

YOUR FIRST HAT

Randi (page 68) and Tore (page 106) and their daughter Talitha are snug and warm in their basic hats, each knit in a color chosen especially for them.

If you have just learned the basics of knitting, I will now walk you through making a very simple hat. The hat here is presented in small, medium, and large sizes. The small size is given first; medium and large sizes follow in parentheses. Specific directions for each size are given in the same sequence throughout the pattern. It can be helpful to go through the pattern first and highlight the directions for the right size, so you don't accidentally knit the wrong number of stitches.

Once you've mastered the basic hat, I will show you how to incorporate a motif, and finally how to create a hat with your own personalized design.

BASIC HAT PATTERN

Size: Small (Medium, Large)

YARN AND NEEDLES

- Size 10½ (6.5mm) 16-inch circular needle and set of 4 or 5 double-pointed needles

- 2 skeins of bulky weight yarn in any color

- I have used Alfa yarn in Pink (4513), Blue (6755), and Brown (3082). You may choose other colors, but if you choose another type of yarn, make sure that it has a gauge of 13 stitches = 4 inches.

GAUGE

13 stitches = 4 inches (10cm) (See page 47 for more on gauge.)

PATTERN

- Start by casting on 54 (60, 66) stitches. Count them to make sure you have 54 (60, 66) before going further.

- Make sure the stitches are not twisted around the needle. Place a marker (to indicate the beginning of the round) and join the work in a circle. Place the needle with the yarn strands in your right hand, and put the working yarn over your left index finger (not the yarn tail).

- Now you're going to knit "ribbing," which helps the hat fit snugly around the head. Starting at the stitch marker (the beginning of the round), knit 1 stitch. Then purl 1 stitch. Then knit 1 stitch again. Keep going around, knitting 1 and then purling 1, until you get back to the stitch marker.

- Do 5 more rounds of ribbing (knit 1, purl 1).

- After 6 rounds of ribbing, stop. If you are incorporating a chart, this is when you start working the stitches in the chart (see page 166). If you are making a plain hat, change to plain knitting or stockinette stitch (knit every stitch). Just keep knitting around and around until your hat measures 3 (4, 4½) inches [9 (10, 11)cm] from the ribbing.

- Now you're going to start decreasing (making the hat smaller), using the Knitkid Decreasing Formula from page 50. The formula is:

$$\frac{\text{number of stitches} - 12}{6} = \begin{array}{l}\text{number} \\ \text{of stitches} \\ \text{between} \\ \text{each} \\ \text{decrease}\end{array}$$

Start by using the formula to calculate the number of stitches between each decrease for your desired hat size.

If you're making a small hat, your formula would look like this:

$$\frac{54 - 12}{6} = \begin{array}{l}7 \text{ stitches} \\ \text{between} \\ \text{each} \\ \text{decrease}\end{array}$$

For a medium hat, it would be:

$$\frac{60 - 12}{6} = \begin{array}{l}8 \text{ stitches} \\ \text{between} \\ \text{each} \\ \text{decrease}\end{array}$$

And for a large hat, it would be:

$$\frac{66 - 12}{6} = \begin{array}{l}9 \text{ stitches} \\ \text{between} \\ \text{each} \\ \text{decrease}\end{array}$$

- Now use your calculation to start the decrease. Start the next round by knitting 2 stitches together (k2tog), then knit 7 (8, 9) stitches, then knit 2 together, then knit 7 (8, 9) stitches. Continue like this all around, with 7 (8, 9) stitches between every decrease (k2tog). When you finish one full round, you will have decreased in six places.

- Knit 1 round without decreasing.

- On the next round you will decrease again. But this time, you'll knit one less stitch between each decrease. Start by knitting 2 together, just as last time. Then knit 6 (7, 8) stitches, knit 2 together, knit 6 (7, 8). Continue this way all around.

- Work 1 round without decreasing.

- Do another decrease round, again knitting one less stitch between each decrease. Knit 2 together, knit 5 (6, 7), knit 2 together, knit 5 (6, 7), and so on. (You will now be able to more clearly see the places where you have decreased on the hat.)

- Continue like this until you have done five rounds with decreasing and five rounds without decreasing (10 rounds total).

- Now start decreasing on every round, skipping the regular rounds in between.

(continued on next page)

- Continue until your circular needles are too long to hold the few stitches remaining. Then switch to double-pointed needles (DPNs). (See page 161 for more on using DPNs.) Keep decreasing until you have only 6 stitches left.

- To finish, cut the yarn leaving an 8-inch (20cm) tail. Pull the tail through the remaining stitches and draw tightly to close the top of your hat.

- Weave in the yarn ends with a yarn needle.

- Congratulations, you have finished your first hat. I am proud of you.

ADDING A DESIGN

You can take the basic hat shown on page 164 a step further by using the same basic pattern and adding a personalized design, which is conveyed in a chart. Here I'll walk you through the basic steps of incorporating a chart.

Motifs are difficult to present in more than one size, so this pattern was created for the medium size hat only.

Åse wears the basic hat with a simple checkerboard design. Adding a design to the basic hat pattern is the first step to designing your own hats.

YARN AND NEEDLES

- Size 8 (5mm) 16-inch circular needles

- Size 10½ (6.5mm) 16-inch circular needles and set of 4 or 5 double-pointed needles

- 3 skeins of bulky weight yarn, 2 Main Color, and 1 Contrasting Color. I have used Alfa yarn in Blue (6755) as main color and White (1012) as contrast color. You may choose other colors. But if you choose another type of yarn, just make sure that it has the gauge 13 stitches = 4 inches.

GAUGE

13 stitches = 4 inches (10cm)

PATTERN

- Start by casting on 60 stitches onto the smaller needle. Count them to make sure you have the correct number, then place a marker (to indicate the beginning of the round) and join the work in a circle.

TIP Using a smaller size needle for the ribbing makes the ribbing a little more snug.

- Follow the Basic Hat Pattern until you have finished the 6 rounds of ribbing, working either a knit 1/purl 1 ribbing as shown on page 164, or the knit 2/purl 2 ribbing shown here.

- Then take the larger needle in your right hand and knit the whole work onto this needle using only knit stitches. The ribbing is now finished, and you are ready to start working the chart.

- Look at the chart. You will always read the chart from right to left, beginning at the bottom with Row 1. Note that you have to knit the first stitch with the main color (blue). Attach your contrast color (white) (see "joining new yarn" on page 162). Making sure to knit with the working yarn end (not the tail end), knit 2 stitches. Now grasp the main color and knit 2 stitches. The whole first round is a loop going like this: One blue, two white, two blue, two white, one blue, two white.

- Reading the chart from right to left, you'll see that the second and third rounds go like this: Three blue, two white, three blue, two white.

- Continue working through the chart. When you have knit all the rows, cut the white yarn (leaving a short tail for weaving in). Then just go back to knitting all the stitches in blue.

- Keep knitting around until the work measures 4 inches (10cm) from the top of the ribbing.

- Continue as in the Basic Hat Pattern from the decrease.

- Congratulations! You finished your first hat with a design.

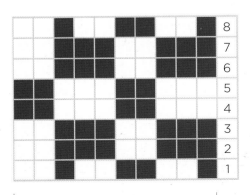

— 10-STITCH REPEAT —

DESIGNING YOUR OWN UNIQUE HAT

Designing a personalized hat for someone is what this project has been all about. I have been inspired by the people around me. First I vaguely imagine a certain hat on a certain person, and then I follow this vague picture, and start experimenting. When the hat is done, it is quite rewarding to see it on the head of the person who first inspired me. And of course, the person who receives it is very happy.

Is there someone you want to bring some happiness to, someone who inspires you to design a unique hat? Try to imagine what kind of colors and design would look good on that person, and go to work. When you extend a little handmade warmth to someone, whether friend or stranger, it will make both of you happy. I guarantee it.

Personalizing a hat with your own design is easier than you might think. Start with a piece of graph paper, a pencil, some colored pencils, and a ruler.

Each square on the graph paper represents one stitch. You are going to make a pattern by filling in squares to form a design. This is the design, or "motif," that will be repeated around your hat.

1. The first step is to figure out how large your motif can be—meaning how many stitches (or squares) wide, and how many rows (or squares) high. There is one rule: the number of stitches in one repeat of your motif must divide evenly into the number of stitches cast on for the hat.

If you're designing a motif to use with the Basic Hat Pattern on page 165, just follow these simple guidelines:

For a small hat (54 stitches cast on), your motif can be 6 or 9 stitches (or squares) wide and 8 to 15 rows high.

For a medium hat (60 stitches cast on), your motif can be 6, 10, 12, or 15 stitches (squares) wide and 8 to 15 rows high.

For a large hat (66 stitches cast on), your motif can be 6 or 11 stitches (squares) wide and 8 to 15 rows high.

2. Choose a width and height for your motif and mark off the appropriate number of squares on graph paper. Remember, each square going across (from right to left) is one stitch. Each row of squares going up (from bottom to top) is one row of knitting.

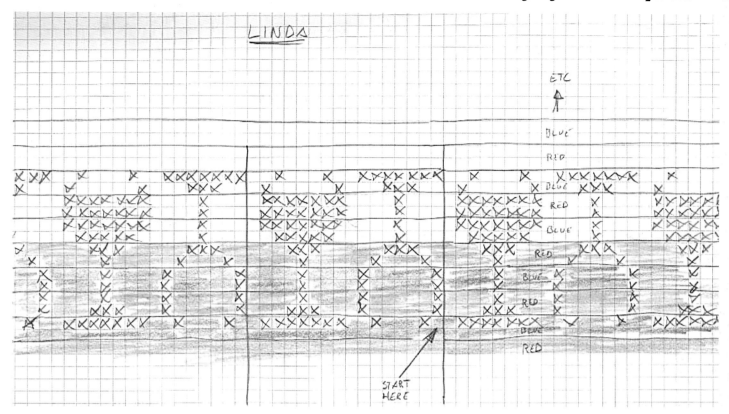

Here's an example of how I designed the motif for Linda's hat (on page 150). I knew I wanted it to have wine glasses so I drew those first, alternating them right side up and upside down, using x's to create the design. Then I chose the background colors and filled those in with colored pencils. Because the background colors are dark, I decided to knit the wine glasses in white.

3. Fill in the squares with a motif. Try creating a design with simple shapes, like circles, squares, and lines. Don't forget to include an empty square or two on the end if you want spaces between the repeats. Then use colored pencils to decide which color yarn you'll use for each stitch. (For tips on creating a motif, see pages 170-171.) For your first design, I recommend starting with only knit stitches. But once you're comfortable, try playing around with patterns of knit and purl stitches, using a different symbol in the squares for each, such as "blank" for knit and "–" for purl.

4. To see how many times you'll repeat your motif around the hat, divide the number of stitches/squares it is wide into the number of stitches cast on. For example, if you're making a medium hat and your motif is 10 stitches wide, divide 60 by 10 = 6 times around. If you're making a large hat and your motif is 6 stitches wide, divide 66 by 6 = 11 times around. You might want to go ahead and draw that number of repeats, so you can see the entire series of repeats laid out.

5. Now simply swap your chart for the one in the Basic Hat pattern, and you're ready to start knitting.

You can also use the instructions here to create a personalized motif for any of the patterns in this book. Just look at the chart that accompanies the pattern and make your own motif the same number of squares wide and high. Before you know it, you'll have created your own unique, one-of-a-kind, never-before-seen, ready-to-be-unleashed hat. ✤

THAT HAT IS SO YOU

Making a hat that suits the person it's intended for is part of the creativity of the Knitting Project. So how do you create the right hat for someone? The two big decisions are color(s) and design.

What color? When I design a hat, I first consider the color of the person's eyes. Then I look at hair color, skin color, and the colors of their clothes. These are all visual clues that tell me which colors will work in their hat. I quite often choose a color that matches the person's eye color. Look at the portraits in this book and you'll see that many blue-eyed people have received blue hats. When it comes to hair, I generally like choosing some kind of blue for blond people, and maybe brown or beige for people with darker hair. If a person has dark-colored skin, I like using pure black as main color, and then adding strong contrasting colors like white and red. Warm colors, like orange, beige, and red, also work with dark-colored skin. Some colors, like green, work fine with many types of coloring.

You can also use color to emphasize personality type. Red hats work very well on passionate people. For example, Ingrid Elin has quite a temper and is a kick boxer, so I made her a hat the color of fire and action. Maria is passionate, too, but she is also quite feminine, so I added pink to hers.

What design? Some people are lively, some introverted, some thoughtful and philosophical, some mild and empathetic, some "hard" and scientific. All these things determine what their headwear should look like. In some cases you can be very concrete: I knew that Tobias loves tractors and

TOBIAS

GULLEIV

INGRID ELIN

Gulleiv is a bass player, so deciding on the design for their hats was easy. But normally you have to think in more abstract ways. If a person is quiet and empathic, you might want to put soft circular motifs on the hat. If he is a very logical person, you might use squares or angles. A lively person might get a more complex design, while a quiet and introverted person would get a simpler hat design.

Remember: When it comes to making a hat suit a person, there are no rules. I have only given you some guidelines that I have found useful in my work. So just go ahead and experiment. It's only a hat, after all, and it's only knitting!

MARIA

ACKNOWLEDGMENTS

THANKS TO ALL THE PEOPLE WHO HELPED MAKE THIS BOOK POSSIBLE.

KLAUS NILSEN SKRUDLAND, the photographer

ÅSE TAKVAM, my girlfriend and the technical advisor in the initial phases

JULIE MAZUR and LINDA HETZER, the editors

GOODESIGN, the designer

SVEIN KÅRE GUNNARSON, for designing the charts

JARED FLOOD, for inspiration and for help with the patterns

HEIDI STRAUME, for helping me with the text

ØRJAN ABELSNES, for building the Knitkid stand

PER KÅRE REIERSEN (at Fasett), for creating the Knitkid logo
and for inspiring the design of the book

JENS OLAV HETLAND, for designing the Knitkid stand

ÅSHILD LUNDETRÆ FIDJE, the technical supervisor and my inspiration

KOLBJØRN AKERVOLD, the head of Dale Yarn a/s

SANDNES YARN A/S, yarn manufacturer

STEINAR ENGELSEN, photographer of the family pictures

INGVILD AARSLAND, photographer of the portraits of Åse
and Ingeborg and my author photo, among others

STAVANGER KOMMUNE, my city, for financial support

LEIF JOHAN SEVLAND, the mayor, for his desire to receive one of my hats